auf Wiedersehen

WWII Through the Eyes of a German Girl

Christa Holder Ocker

Published by Rogue Phoenix Press
Second Addition
Copyright © 2014

Characters and incidents depicted in this book are products of the author's personal knowledge, experiences, and memories. No part of this book may be reproduced or transmitted in any form or by any means, electronic or mechanical, including photocopying, recording, or by any information storage and retrieval system, without permission in writing from the publisher.

ISBN: 978-1-62420-144-8

Credits
Cover Artist: Designs by Ms. G
Editor: Sherry Derr-Wille

Dedication

For my son Peter Wolfgang Ocker
1965 – 2003
In Remembrance

Acknowledgments

To the Silk Purse Writer's Group - Laura Pelner McCarthy, Judy Reene Singer, Maria Gil, Laura Liller, Linda Gould, Lynn Hoines, and Debra Scacciaferro – many thanks for your passionate attention and diagnostic advice. Special thanks to Arlene Mandell, dear friend.

1

"When will we come back?" my sister asked, an edge of desperation in her voice.

Mutti stopped in the open doorway, turned around, and as if to avoid the question, she pointed to the distant wall. "Look *Kinder*," she whispered.

A shaft of sun found its way through the ice-laced window, spilling its silvery light on the painting above the couch, illuminating the wake on a river flowing still.

Sadness crept into my heart as my eyes returned to my mother, so tall, so graceful, her ash-blond hair knotted in a bun at the nape of her neck. A tear rolled down her high cheekbone. She wiped it away with her fingertips, then closed the door with a decisive click.

~ * ~

For as long as I could remember, this had been our home, a happy home filled with laughter and song. The apartment, gracious and inviting, furnished with unassuming elegance, was located on the first floor of a new apartment building on the outskirts of Görlitz, in the eastern part of Germany. The luscious aroma from *Frau* Ömichen's

auf Wiedersehen

kitchen on the second floor still lingered in the stairway, and her deep foghorn voice resounded off the granite walls, *Komm rauf,* Christa, *wir haben Kartoffel Plinse...*Günter *warted auf Dich.* Come upstairs, Christa, we're having potato pancakes. Günter is waiting for you. Günter, at six, one year younger than I, was her only son and my friend and playmate.

A while back, wanting a baby brother, Günter convinced me, although I already had an older sister, I should have a little brother too. So we left cottage cheese sandwiches on our windowsills. Everyone knew, of course, the stork brought a baby if you left him a cottage cheese sandwich on the windowsill, at least in our part of Germany. One day, soon after, Günter came skipping downstairs. "Guess what..." his voice danced ahead of him. "I'm going to get a little baby brother."

I looked at *Mutti,* anticipation rising to explosion force, but she shook her head from side to side.

"I knew it," I stamped my foot, both hands on my hips. "You didn't put enough cottage cheese on the bread." I was upset. "*Frau Ömichen* put on a lot more."

"Well, that's because Günter's *Vati* was on furlough, you know, and they got extra rations," she sputtered through giggles. Both our fathers were off, fighting Hitler's war.

Yes, it had been a happy home and I, wrapped in a silken cocoon of a child's ignorance, was oblivious to the evil and destruction all around us. Still, there were scenes that penetrated the walls of my cocoon and I could not deny the dull ache of foreboding, as on one cold glacial day...

~ * ~

A truculent wind blew across the land and covered the streets in white. Tugging at my arm, my mother urged, "*Komm, lauf schneller.* Come, walk faster." Hunched against winter's wrath, weighted down with Christmas gifts, we pushed on toward my grandmother's house when, through the silence of the snow, a scream split early dusk. A clock from a nearby steeple struck five. Through curtains of flurries people, like phantoms, approached. Their eyes to the ground, they passed us by without a sound. Soldiers herded the group along with rifles and whips shouting, "*Weiter Jude, los, mach schnell.* Move on, Jew, get going, quick." And the wind shoved and slashed against the damned, singing a sorrowful song. Barely a shadow away, caught in the shaft of light falling from a street lamp, one of them not much older than I raised her head and looked my way, eyes dark and deep alive with fear held on to mine. Suspended in a surreal nightmare, I willed her to come with us…

~ * ~

"When will we come back, *Mutti*?" My sister's question, more persistent this time, cut through the fog.

"Some day, perhaps…." *Mutti*'s smile transformed her face into thought as she glanced at my sister. "Or maybe we'll go to America." She turned the brass key in the lock, and then buried it in the bottom of her knapsack. "I have a friend in America," she continued, pulling us toward the old Wehrmacht truck parked in front of our building. "Maybe I can locate him…maybe he'll help us…"

"America?" The soldier, a willowy figure in splendid boots, carrying our two bags, all the belongings we could manage, looked over his shoulder, raising his eyebrows in question. "Can I come along?" He hauled the bags into the truck and, not waiting for an answer, he retreated to the front. We struggled to climb aboard, hindered by the layers and layers of clothes we wore that had not fit into the bags. It was a day near the beginning of February of 1945, World War II was drawing

auf Wiedersehen

to an end, and we were fleeing westward before the onrushing Red Army. The request 'All mothers and children go west' had come several days earlier, but I had been in bed with a fever, developed from a festering wound. A wound sustained, one day, from a fall after playing with Günter upstairs. Almost every day I went upstairs to play with my friend. *Frau* Ömichen, his mother, didn't mind so much when we messed up their place. Their place was, more often than not, a bit untidy anyway, with all the artifacts scattered about, collecting dust. At the end of a play date when *Mutti* called, I always went home by schussing down the banister. On that fateful day, however, I had leaned over too far and, instead of sliding, went flying head first, cracking my chin wide open. When the army trucks arrived for the transport west, my fever had climbed to 105°. Luckily, Günter's mother was also my mother's best friend, and they stayed with us until the fever broke, and another truck came for us.

~ * ~

"Over here," *Frau* Ömichen now called as we climbed in. Just then the streetcar came clanking by. I squinted my eyes to see if I could recognize the conductor, to see if he was the same conductor who scolded Günter and me one day last summer, when we placed some stones on the rails. The streetcar stopped, and the conductor came rushing at us waving his index finger shouting "*Verdammte Kinder,* I'll have your hide." Our mothers gave us 'room arrest' for one whole week. It was still a puzzle to me, for all we wanted to do was flatten a few stones. A few flat stones so we could make them skip in the rainwater puddles behind our home. Of course, I knew we weren't supposed to go into the street, but...

"Over here," *Frau* Ömichen called again over the noise of the streetcar passing by, and waved her big pudgy hand.

The truck was filled with people, mostly older folks, a few other mothers and kids, all strangers. Günter came scrambling toward us and took my hand, leading us to their corner.

"*Pass auf,* Watch out," an old man grumbled when I accidentally stepped on his outstretched legs.

Rosel, my sister, sniveled as we huddled close in the shadows of the truck, trying to keep warm. I was okay, though. Hearing Günter's whisper in my ear "You're my bestest friend," helped a lot. Besides, we were going to America, the place of milk and honey. My stomach grumbled. "I'm hungry," I said. Just then, the soldier approached the back of the truck and pulled the canopy down. We sat in silence and in darkness, until the engine sputtered to life and the truck started to roll over snow-powdered cobblestone streets, farther and farther west, farther and farther away from home.

2

Someone was playing the harmonica. My consciousness clouded in half-sleep, I listened and recognized the familiar tune. The player skipped a note or two, whenever the driver hit a pothole. There was no mistaking, it was a tune my father had often played, a tune he had taught me how to play. I started to hum along. Soon someone else joined in. Then someone else, and still someone else, until all the people in the truck joined in either humming or singing the words, *muß i' denn, muß i' denn zum Städtele hinaus, Städtele hinaus und Du mein Schatz bleibst hier.* Got to go, got to go, got to leave this town, leave this town and you, my dear, stay here.

A feeling of happiness arose inside me with the memory of *Vati*, my father, closing in. I shut my eyes, trying to remember his face. His face was lost, no longer in focus. When was the last time I had seen *Vati*? I tried to force his likeness on my mind, but could not. Weary, I dreamed of a man in a sailor's suit, with a shock of wavy black hair, playing the harmonica. A faceless man, except for the mouth blowing into a harmonica, and then he disappeared altogether.

"Wake up, wake up." Rosel pulled on my coat sleeve, "We have to go."

"Go where?" I rubbed my eyes and looked at *Mutti*, my mother, who was already picking up our two bags.

"Don't ask holes in your stomach." She smiled. "Just follow us."

Not yet adjusted to wakefulness, I scrambled up and stumbled behind her. Günter and his mother were already climbing off the truck with the help of the soldier. The soldier, in his splendid boots, pointed into the distance, to a warehouse next to a railroad station. With darkness pressing down on us, we staggered toward our stay for the night.

~ * ~

"Tomorrow," *Mutti* ran the bristle brush through my sister's long golden Hair, "we'll get on a train that will take us to Apolda..."

"Where? Ouch." Rosel winced in pain as the brush got caught on a tangle.

"Apolda…it's a lovely town." *Mutti* tried to disentangle the brush from my sister's hair. Having succeeded, she paused for a moment then added in a voice that seemed to come from a long way off, "You'll like it there." With her fingers tightening on the grip of the brush, she continued with her long, decisive strokes. She was convinced the only way to keep us louse free in this cold dreary mausoleum of a building, filled with straw for hundreds of people to sleep on, was to keep brushing our hair, and she focused on this ritual with utmost concentration. It was her pride throughout life that we never contracted lice, not even in the overnight refugee camp.

"Where is Apolda?" my sister asked through tight lips, holding a bobby-pin between her teeth.

"It's not far…it's west of here," said *Frau* Ömichen, nestling her corpulent frame next to us.

auf Wiedersehen

"Where?" Rosel persisted.

"Away from those damn Russians." *Frau* Ömichen emphasized damn by raising her voice.

"What's a damn Russian, *Mutti*?" I asked.

"Shush." She stroked my head. "Never mind…go to sleep…everything will be fine."

She was doing a lot of shushing lately, but it always worked and I went to sleep dreaming of a train ride that took us to Apolda, where all the houses were filled with the scent of *Frau* Ömichen's *Kartoffel Plinse*.

~ * ~

It was the night of February 13th, and in a city not far from us, in the medieval city of Dresden, the screams of thousands were silenced while sucked into the red glow of a firestorm.

On this night the RAF, and on the following two days the United States Air Force, dropped clusters of combustible bombs on Dresden, creating huge fires. With the flash of heated air roaring toward the sky, and cold air rushing in at ground level, a huge suction was formed that raged through the streets with immense force, disposing of everything in its way, thus spreading the fire still further and further until it became a typhoon. All human effort was useless. The panic-stricken people, driven from their shelter by flames, were sucked up like rag dolls. Those scurrying back into their shelters suffocated before being reduced to ashes.

The intention of the attack, according to an internal Royal Air Force memo, was 'to hit the enemy where he feels it most'. Dresden was a cultural city, Germany's seventh largest city, overflowing at this time with refugees pouring westward, mostly women, children, old men, and returning wounded soldiers.

Christa Holder Ocker

~ * ~

"No, don't look." *Mutti* pushed us back, away from the train windows, trying to shield the view with her body. Our train slowed to a crawl and the people stepped out of their compartments into the passageway, to look out the windows facing what had been Dresden. A ghostly hush fell over the train as it chugged its way, in slow motion, through the ruins. Several times, it stopped altogether, a few old men would scramble off and clear the tracks. Even *Frau* Ömichen, for once, was speechless, but then turning to my mom she wiped her cheek with the back of her hand and whispered, "Do you realize had it not been for Christa's fever, we would have passed through here a week ago? We would have been inside the inferno." An overpowering odor permeated the air, and someone down the passageway rasped, "It's smoldering flesh."

I squeezed my head between people's hips, and narrowed my eyes straining to see, smoke was the only movement in a gray cloud of dust. With my throat tightening, I returned to my seat, next to Günter. He took my hand and held on tight.

~ * ~

I wondered if Görlitz, our city, had been bombed too. If *Frau* Mueller's beautiful white stucco house was reduced to a black cinder box. *Frau* Mueller's house stood in a row of neat houses, which we always passed on the way to the house of my grandmother, *Oma* Holder. It wasn't an ordinary house. The stucco exterior was smoother and whiter than all the others. That was the reason I think, why I had chosen it to be the recipient of my creative work. While walking behind my mother and sister one late afternoon, I took the thick blue crayon I found on the sidewalk a block before, and went up and down, and up and down, all along the façade, creating beautiful ocean waves, so blue. *Frau* Mueller had not liked my ocean waves. She came storming out the front door, waving her index finger, shouting, "*Du Lausebub*, I'll get you." I wondered why she called me a lousy boy. With my long chestnut pigtails anyone could tell I was a girl, and besides, like all girls I wore a dress. Then she started to pull my ear, back and forth, as if she wanted to yank it off. Hearing the commotion, *Mutti* turned around and, with my sister in tow, faced the enraged woman while snatching me out of her grasp. Like two bulls, with puffs of steam coming out of their noses, they vented their anger and frustration.

"Why do you carry on so, *dumme Frau*?" my mother yelled, flinging her arm into the air. "Soon enough the Russians will seize your precious little house, and then what difference will it make?" We left poor *Frau* Mueller standing on the sidewalk with her mouth wide open, and I, my arm still trapped by Mutti's iron hand, got the biggest lecture regarding respect for other people's property, all the way to my grandmother's house.

~ * ~

"Do you want some bread?" *Frau* Ömichen, who seemed able to produce something to eat by sheer magic, snapped me out of my thoughts, waving a piece of bread under my nose. "Do you want a piece of bread?" she repeated, drawing her thick bushy eyebrows together.

"*Nein*." For once I was not hungry. Günter started to cough, trying to swallow the piece of bread stuck in his throat. He was beginning to turn blue when *Frau* Ömichen slapped him hard between the shoulder blades, and the piece of bread popped out. *Mutti* remained motionless by the window, even as the train started to pick up speed again, leaving Dresden behind. At last, with shoulders drooping, she came back into our compartment and fell into her seat. Hugging herself, she stared into nothingness. I didn't ask her anything. I sensed this time she would not shush me, she would not say don't worry, she would not say everything is fine. So I took her long- fingered strong hand into mine and stroked it, again and again.

3

A wind light and sweet welcomed us as we stepped off the train at the Apolda *Bahnhof*. The railroad station, except for a few travelers hastening by, was deserted at this early hour. No sooner had we disembarked, our train chugged back to life with the locomotive erupting in smoke and the whistle squealing its farewell. Standing there on the platform, with all our possessions in the two bags at our feet, we watched the train wind its way out of the station, and wondered what to do next.

"*Heil* Hitler." A youth, with cheeks still rosy like a child's, greeted us. His arm, sporting the familiar red armband with its swastika signifying he belonged to the Hitler Youth, shot up in the straight-arm Nazi salute. "Can I be of help?"

"*Guten Morgen.*" *Mutti* smiled with one side of her mouth. She never did get accustomed to the Nazi greeting, and often she received cold stares of admonition from neighbors and friends when she greeted them with a warm "*Guten Morgen*, or *Guten Tag*, or *Guten Abend*. Good morning, good day, good evening." Even *Vati*, my father, scolded her once, back in Görlitz...

His hands clasped behind his back, *Vati* paced up and down our living room floor, letting his foot come down hard on the board that creaked. With a sudden stop, he stood riveted, faced *Mutti*, and in a voice edged with disapproval asked, "Why won't you say *Heil* Hitler? Do you want me to lose my place in the *Kapelle*? Do you not like the extra money it brings in?"

Besides playing the harmonica, *Vati* played the trumpet in a band, a Nazi band, I think. *Mutti*, although realizing he'd joined not just for the need of money, but also for the love of music, straightened her shoulders and, almost towering over him, said in a low matter-of-fact voice, "Why don't you shave that stupid little mustache?" Wounded by her words, *Vati* threw back his head, unclasped his hands from behind his back, placed them on his hips, and pranced about like a peacock in rut, mumbling something about a stubborn East Prussian. *Mutti* was born in Königsberg, East Prussia.

We stood like posts, Rosel and I, waiting and watching in the shadows, when a giggle escaped my sister's lips, and then one more, and one more until I began to giggle too. Stunned, *Vati* froze in his peacock dance and glared at us, but then his lips parted in a dazzling display of white teeth and he joined us in laughter. Even *Mutti* laughed too, but her eyes were not laughing. Her eyes remained sad...

~ * ~

My father did have a mustache. I saw it on the photograph *Mutti* kept in a locket between her breasts, the one she pulled out whenever he threatened to become faceless again. A square little mustache that adorned so many fathers' faces in the Third Reich, including, of course, the face of the *Führer* of our *Vaterland*, Hitler's face, the mad man's face.

auf Wiedersehen

~ * ~

"Perhaps..." *Mutti* fumbled in her coat pocket and pulled out a crumpled sheet of paper. Pulling at the edges to get the creases out, she handed it to the youth. "Perhaps you can tell us where this place is?"

"Let me see." The youth, with his childlike rosy cheeks, spread his legs in a stance of importance and, holding his chin in the V of his forefinger and thumb as if unraveling evolution, waited for a sign of admiration. Realizing we were not impressed, he pointed down the street. "That way...*ja*, just go all the way down that street, then turn left at the end."

"*Dankeschön.* Thank you." *Mutti* took the crumpled sheet of paper and put it back in her pocket.

In acknowledgement the youth clicked his heels together, which made *Mutti* smile with half a mouth again. Then he turned to *Frau* Ömichen who handed him her address.

I tried to click my heels together, but no matter how hard and how quick I brought them together, my shoes, handed down to me from my sister, were worn, and did not click. Günter, on the other hand, could make his heels click and did so without pause, until *Frau* Oehmichen, who by now also found out which way to go, pulled his ear and told him to stop.

The squeal of a whistle drifting in on the warm spring-like wind, and puffs of white smoke billowing in the distance, announced the arrival of another train. The Hitler Youth left our midst and standing at attention, faced the incoming train and saluted a German officer who was jumping off the still moving staff car. As soon as the train came to a full stop, the doors opened and, as if in slow motion one by one, men in rumpled uniforms emerged, men with one leg, men with one arm, men with one eye, men with blood and pus oozing through their dirty bandages. Soon the deserted railroad platform was swarming with staggering wretched men, remnants of Hitler's victorious *Wehrmacht*. I searched their faces wondering if *Vati*, my father, might be among them, but their uniforms were different. My father was somewhere on a battleship.

"They're coming from the Russian front," *Frau* Ömichen said through quivering lips. "Look what those damn Russians did to them." As her eyes darted from face to face, she breathed a sigh of relief, again and again, until she was confident Günter's father was not among them. Herr Ömichen was fighting at the Russian front. She had not heard from him in a very long time.

"Why did those damn Russians hurt them, *Mutti*?" I asked.

"Shush…don't worry…they'll be all right." *Mutti* flashed a look of reproach her friend's way, then quickly picked up our bags and nudged us off the platform, my sister and me, through the pitiful crowd and outside. *Frau* Ömichen and Günter followed close behind.

It was time to say *auf Wiedersehen*. Günter and his mother's new temporary home was located, according to the Hitler youth's direction and to our disappointment, on the opposite side of town.

The two women hugged again and again. Then grasping Rosel's thick blond braids, *Frau* Ömichen pulled her close, and planted a kiss with her ample lips on my sister's mouth. Rosel's nose wrinkled up. Next, it was my turn. *Frau* Ömichen buried my face in her pendulous breasts and rocked us back and forth, back and forth. When at last she stopped, Günter, who with his head tilted, stood very still, came over and gave me a buzz on my cheek. I gripped his two shoulders and returned the buzz. After all, we were going to be married one day. It didn't bother me he was a year younger and almost a head shorter. He had a dimple in his chin, and his eyes twinkled when he smiled, that was nice. Besides, we got along just fine, and on occasion told our mothers "When we are married, you cannot tell us anymore what to do."

"Don't forget." *Frau* Ömichen wiped her cheek with the back of her hand. "Come and visit as soon as you can."

"*Ja,* of course...I wish I could be there when the baby arrives." *Mutti's* brows drew together in concern. "How much longer did you say?"

"I think real soon." *Frau* Ömichen chuckled. "The way it's been kicking...maybe today." When she saw the crease between *Mutti's* brows deepening, she quickly added, "*Nein, nein*...I'm kidding. It's not due for a while."

At last, we parted and headed in opposite directions.

"Good luck with your plans for America," *Frau* Ömichen yelled over her shoulder. "Let me know how you make out."

Stumbling backwards, we waved and waved to each other, Günter and I, until he rounded a corner and disappeared from sight.

4

"*Guten Morgen.*" My mother struggled with her coat pocket and pulled out a sheet of paper. "Is this the right address?"

"*Ja*...this is the address you're looking for." The lady of the Villa, dressed in a pencil slim cashmere suit, held the door open, half way. With the back of her hand pressed to her forehead, she looked us up and down through ice blue eyes that almost disappeared in her taut bony cheeks. I wondered if she had a headache. I remembered Mutti with that same pained expression, one time when Vati, my father, came home on furlough. *Mutti* suffered from a severe headache. *That must be it*, I thought. *That is why the lady greeted us not with warmth, but with disdain.*

We followed the lady's stiff back, with her silver head held high, through an immense marble entryway, up a wide maroon deep-carpeted stairway, and down a narrow dark corridor with many closed doors. She stopped in front of one of the closed doors, jammed a long brass key into the bolt, and unlocked it. Half turning, she pointed down the long hallway. "That's the lavatory. You'll have to share it with the other...hmm...refugees on this floor." A flicker of a smile rose at the edges of her mouth, as if to soften the word refugees, but it quickly died when she heard me say. "I have to pee." I held my hands between my legs.

This made the back of her hand go up to her forehead again, and she retreated.

We stepped into our room, small and dark except for a shaft of sun streaming through the window on the far wall. Mutti dropped the bags and collapsed unto one of the two narrow beds. Besides the beds, there was a table with two chairs, and a credenza with an electric two-burner plate. The room was dense with the smell of mildew and neglect, so I walked to the window and opened it wide.

"Oh, *Mutti*." I was spellbound. "Come and see." Stretched out below was the most magnificent garden I had ever seen, trees majestic, even in their barren state, and pebbled walk-ways leading around a still fountain to a gazebo in the far corner. *Mutti* and Rosel came to the window and drew in the brisk February air.

"Look…" my mother pointed to the Gazebo. A group of children had gathered there. "Christa, why don't you go and say hello." She waved me on with a flip of her hand. "Go…go…Rosel, you run along too."

My sister shook her head from side to side. She always stayed very close to Mutti.

I was anxious to make new friends, but it was of utmost urgency I visit the lavatory first. So I hurried down the narrow corridor, and turned the knob, but the door was locked. I knocked. A muffled grunt was the response. So I knocked again, and again, and again, until at last an elderly man emerged, a journal tucked under his arm. He held an empty bucket in one hand. "*Blöde Gans*", he mumbled, shuffling past me. I didn't like being called a 'stupid goose'.

Small like a closet, the lavatory had a narrow curtained window, a toilet, and a sink. Relieved, I looked for paper. I craned my neck as far back as I could, first one way, than the other, but there was no toilet paper. So I did the best I could by wiggling up and down to dispense of any droplets.

When I pulled the chain connected to the small tank up on the wall above the toilet, it didn't flush. I pulled again, harder this time, but it still didn't flush. I opened the faucet on the sink, a spurt of brown water spit out, then nothing at all, and someone banged on the door. With my hands unwashed, my eyes to the floor, I escaped and found my way downstairs, through a back door leading to the garden, past the fountain, to the gazebo.

"Hey there…are you the new kid?" A boy, his hair the color of field oats, pushed through the group of boys and girls and took a step toward me. "What's your name?"

"Christa," I said and hooked my thumbs in my coat pockets trying to look nonchalant.

"I'm Klaus," he said. "I live over there." He pointed to the huge villa next door. Then, indicating the other children with a jerk of his head and pointing to our villa, he said, "They all live here." Our villa, although somewhat weather-beaten, still had an aura of grandeur, loftiness. These girls and boys, all within a foot of each other's height, were, I could see, refugees like me. Refugees that the lady of the villa and her husband, an elderly man who always appeared bowed down and overwhelmed with burdens, had been forced to take in.

"So…what are you doing?" I asked, noticing that Klaus was the only one here, who, was not dressed in patched clothes. Both my woolen stockings were neatly interweaved at the knees to fill in the holes.

"We're playing war…want to play?"

"Sure…what side should I be on?"

"You can be on my side." With a toss of his head, Klaus flung his hair back bringing to light two smiling eyes, as blue as the clear sky. "We're the Americans, and we're winning."

"Who are they?" I asked, pointing to a group of kids standing in back of the make-believe Americans.

"Oh...they're the Russians, and they're losing." He grinned.

"Where are the Germans?" I asked.

They seemed stumped until the smallest in the Russian group stepped forward and raised his hand as if in school. "I know...I know..."

Everyone turned to him waiting for an answer.

"They all froze dead in Siberia."

"*Halt die Schnauze*." A bigger boy, his brother I presumed, cupped his hand over the little one's mouth.

Not to be silenced, the little one mumbled through his brother's cupped hand, "They did so...I heard *Grossmutter* say so."

"I don't like to play war," I said. "Can't we play something else?"

"You could bring your puppets," one of the older girls suggested to Klaus.

"*Nein*," he pushed his lower lip forward. "I don't like to play with my puppets." When he saw the smile go from my face, he asked "Would you like that?

As the new kid in the garden, it seemed, I received special recognition with special privileges.

"*Ja*, of course." I felt my lips make a smile again. "We could have a puppet show."

"We could sell tickets and make money," the older girl joined in.

"Good, you can have my puppets then. You be in charge of putting on a show." Klaus stressed each word with a tap of his finger on my chest.

"*Ja*, I..."

"Christa-a-a-..." My mother's call interrupted any further plans.

"I have to go... till later..."

"Come back tomorrow," Klaus yelled. "I'll bring my puppets. You can have them."

~ * ~

"We have to get water." My mother held two pails in each hand. "You'll have to come with us."

"Why do I have to go?" I wailed. "Can't I stay and play?"

"Don't always ask holes in your stomach." *Mutti's* voice rang with command. "Just come." When she spoke again, her voice softened. "You have to help us carry the water. Later you can play more with your new friends. Are they nice?" Without waiting for an answer she marched ahead, and Rosel and I followed.

~ * ~

There was a long line of people, mostly women and children carrying empty pails, winding up to the water pump on top of a knoll in the neighboring yard, one of a few remaining water sources still spouting water in our neighborhood. Even though Apolda was spared from firebombs, much was in ill repair including much of the town's water supply. According to *Mutti*, Apolda was spared from the bombs because God did not want the best church bell plant destroyed. After all, some of the finest church steeple bells in the world came from Apolda, including the one in the Cologne Cathedral, which, despite a number of direct hits from Allied bombs, managed to survive when most of Cologne was in ruins.

It was a balmy day in February, almost like spring, and people in the line, glad to be alive, exchanged pleasantries.

auf Wiedersehen

"Where are you from? Where are you staying? Is it not a lovely day?" All of a sudden up in the sky two twin-engine propeller planes, a German Messerschmitt and a British Spitfire, confronted each other with guns blasting away. They dove, and they circled, and they chased each other up and down, their guns spitting fire, rat-tat-tat-tat, rat-tat-tat-tat, right over our heads. The people dove for cover, behind bare bushes, in shallow ditches, rat-tat-tat-tat, rat-tat-tat-tat. I was watching in awe those two fighter planes that somehow strayed from their squadrons, when my mother's strong hands flung me to the ground. "Take cover," she yelled, and my empty pail clanked down the hill. Hitting the dirt and gritting the earth between my teeth, I realized at last, one of these planes could become a fiery ball and fall on us, rat-tat-tat-tat, rat-tat-tat-tat. But the two gunners up in those planes were lousy shots. They kept missing each other, rat-tat-tat- tat, rat-tat-tat-tat. Or maybe they were just tired of killing and the German abandoned the 'fly till you die' policy, rat-tat-tat-tat, rat-tat-tat-tat. In the end they went their separate ways, farther and farther, until they became two dots on the blue horizon. At last they were gone.

With a sigh of relief, everyone got up from the ground, brushed off the loam hugging their clothes, and after collecting their dented pails, lined up once more for water.

5

Edged against the flickering candlelight, our shadows danced on the wall in the twilight of our room. "Today we celebrate," *Mutti* announced, ironing out a crease with her hand in the fine linen tablecloth, the one with the pretty flowers, red, yellow, blue, stitched on by hand, the one her mother, our *Oma* Machein, gave to her on her wedding day, and the only one she brought along. *Oma* Machein, from East Prussia, died years before from a lump in her stomach. The lump in her stomach started to grow because *Oma* Machhein liked to eat roasted coffee beans, Mutti claimed. She also alleged our *Oma* Machhein was the first woman in Germany who had her stomach removed and lived without a stomach for quite a while before she died. "It was a medical break through, you know," she often told us.

"What are we celebrating?" I asked, cocking my head to one side.

"We are celebrating life…life in our new home." That familiar gleam of strength in *Mutti's* sapphire eyes shone in the candlelight.

On the electric two-burner plate something was boiling over, making a fizzling sound. Lately, it was always bubbling and fizzling, never sizzling. I circled my lips with the tip of my tongue, remembering the last time I heard the sizzling sound. *Mutti* was frying a Wiener

Schnitzel. Yes, sizzling was definitely better than fizzling. My stomach growled. I was hungry.

"What are we having?" I asked, sitting down on the empty upright suitcase that served as an extra chair.

"Potato soup." My mother smiled. "The lady of the villa was kind enough to give us some potatoes from her cellar."

Rosel brought the rusty spoons to the table and placed them, with much finesse as if it was the finest silverware, next to our plates.

"Tomorrow…" *Mutti*, with both elbows on the table, interlaced her fingers and rested her jaw on her two thumbs. "Tomorrow, we have to get up early. *Frau* Schmidt says there's a baker downtown that will have some bread."

"Who's *Frau* Schmidt?" I asked.

"She's the woman with the two boys who lives down the hall," Rosel explained, followed by a coughing spell, and *Mutti* cast a worried look her way.

"If we get up early enough, we'll be among the first in line and sure to get some bread…maybe even some rolls."

"I want to go and play," I protested.

"You'll have plenty of time afterwards." *Mutti's* expression grew serious. "Listen girls, we'll have to pretend we don't know each other, all right?"

"Why?" Rosel coughed again.

"Hopefully…" *Mutti* gave a forced smile. "That way, we'll each get a loaf of bread. So, Rosel, you stand a few paces ahead of me. Christa, you stand a few paces in back of me, all right? And don't forget, no talking. Pretend we never met."

Rosel drew her eyebrows together in uncertainty.

"If there's a stampede, use your elbows." *Mutti* demonstrated by bringing her forearms up to her chest, jabbing her elbows, first one then the other, outward. "This way you'll keep your space."

Rosel looked skeptical. "What if…"

"Don't fall," *Mutti* cut in. "Move with the crowd…stay in step…that way you won't be pushed down."

I was going to ask what is a stampede, but *Mutti* drew a pretty clear picture, and so I attacked my soup instead.

The soup tasted like water and salt but the nice atmosphere of candlelight and tablecloth lifted our spirits unaware, at this time, outside a small town not far from us…

~ * ~

Outside the town of Weimar, the town where Goethe and Schiller wrote some of the world's finest literary works, the screams of thousands, behind barbed wire securing Buchenwald, reached the far corners of the world, including the US, but the world closed their doors to Jews seeking asylum, including Pope Pius in his holy robe. He remained quiet and read his bible while the German SS continued their task of the 'Final Solution' to the very end by silencing the screams with a gun, with a rope, with starvation, with cremation.

6

"Are you writing to your friend in America?" *Mutti* was curled over the table, her Grecian nose almost touching the writing-pad, her glasses lay idle at arm's length. She sank the tip of her pen into the ink-glass and, concentrating on her writing, she dismissed me with a vague shake of her head.

Every day, when we came home from standing in line for water, or bread, or potatoes, she sat down by the table, deep in thought, and started to write. I didn't mind. I wanted to be with my friends anyway. Most of the time, Rosel, my sister, buried herself in a book. Today curiosity got hold of me and so I raised my voice and asked again, "Are you writing to your friend in America?"

Mutti breathed a sigh of impatience. She put down the pen, and half twisting around in her seat, faced me. "I'm writing to the Red Cross. They located your cousin Hans." She turned back, settled both elbows on the table, steepled her fingers, and looked into space, her voice trailing off. "Hans was shot in the leg…imagine, sixteen years old…and Hitler sends him off to war…when will this madness end?"

I tried to see my cousin in my mind, but we never met, at least not that I recalled. I remembered, though, hearing *Mutti* and *Vati* talk one time…

~ * ~

Hans was the unwed child of Lieschen, *Mutti's* sister. There was another sister, Lotte. Both were older than *Mutti*, but Lieschen was the pretty one, a look-a-like of Snow White, and spoiled rotten by their mother, *Oma* Machein from East Prussia, my grandmother with the lump in her stomach, and later no stomach at all.

"Hans is a love child…tsk…tsk," *Mutti* whis-pered. A handsome boy, everyone adores…tsk…tsk …just like his father.

"What about Bienchen?" *Vati* asked.

"Bienchen," *Mutti* explained, "came later after Lieschen got married. She married a tailor, no longer alive, and they had a girl named Siegrid. Although not pretty at all, Siegrid was a most generous child, always helping around the house, that's why they nicknamed her Bienchen, for busy as a bee."

~ * ~

"They have a lead on Bienchen, too." *Mutti's* sapphire eyes returned from space and found mine. "It seems Bienchen was separated from her mother when they were running from the Russians. I hope they didn't come across the Baltic Sea."

"Why?" Rosel asked, approaching the table, stifling a cough.

A cloud of sadness settled on *Mutti's* face. "A lot of people broke through the ice and drowned."

"Do you think *Tante* Lieschen drowned?" Rosel bit her lower lip.

"*Nein, nein*...I just mean..." A smile found its way through her mask of uncertainty.

"Where will Bienchen go?" I interrupted.

"She's coming here...and so is her brother Hans." *Mutti* sighed. "I'm writing to the Red Cross that they be sent to us." *Mutti* curled over the table, once more, and started to write again. "Go play," she said.

I walked to the door, opened it, and just before I walked out, *Mutti's* voice reached my ears.

"By the way, I did write to my friend in America, last week, we should hear from him very soon."

~ * ~

My heart pounded as I hurried around the fountain, down the garden path. The air was filled with a fresh scent, the way it always was after an April shower. The raindrops, clinging to the tree limbs, glistened in the high sun. I ducked to avoid a collision with a low hanging magnolia branch. Then I saw him. Klaus was waiting by the gazebo together with the other kids. He'd brought his puppets with playhouse and all, just as he promised.

"Hey, Klaus," I shouted, as I approached the group. "Are you sure it's okay with your mother if you give me your puppets?"

"*Ja*...I told you it was," he said, shifting his weight from one foot to the other. He looked so charming in his Lederhosen with his knees scraped red from climbing too many trees.

I picked up one puppet at a time and let my fingertips glide over the carved wooden faces.

"Awesome...they are so smooth," I whispered. The other kids were already setting up the three-sided playhouse with its show window. After much plotting, shouting, and revising, we performed our first puppet show that very day. As twilight fell over the garden, we heard our mothers call. We stored the puppets and playhouse in a wooden crate, beneath the gazebo.

"See you tomorrow." Klaus smiled as he waved *auf Wiedersehen*, walking off with three other boys. "Don't forget we need to rehearse much more before the big show."

The date was not yet set, but we decided to have a puppet show and invite our mothers, our older siblings, and anyone who wanted to come. The tickets, which we had made from old newspapers reserved as a rule for wiping the you-know-what in the lavatory, and costing three *Pfennig* a person, were almost sold out.

"*Ja,* till tomorrow." I waved back and watched as he hurried up the garden path, a shock of blond hair flapping up and down with each stride he took. I think I was in love, again. At least I didn't miss Günter so much anymore. We had no school because of the shortage of fuel, and while the British and the Americans from the West, and the Russians from the East, raced toward Berlin in the big encirclement, we children took refuge and found magic each day in our play by the gazebo in the garden.

~ * ~

"Did you hear the Americans reached Weimar?" I heard the lady of the villa ask my mother in a hushed tone. They hadn't heard me enter. Rooted to the spot by the door, I struggled to hear and understand their words.

"Buchenwald, I hear, is the first concentration camp to be liberated," the lady continued.

"Free at last," *Mutti* whispered. "Those poor, poor souls…at least they're alive…"

auf Wiedersehen

"Yes...and still they are dying."

"What do you mean?" *Mutti* asked.

"Some are just too sick...some can't stomach the rich food the Americans are giving them...some just tired of life...then again, some of them beat camp guards to death."

"*Ach*, it is all so sad..." *Mutti's* eyes gazed out the window. Thick clouds moved in front of the sun and made the day as gray as the ashes concealing Hitler's bunker in Berlin.

"Some of them..." the lady went on with a sigh, "after they were done with the guards, dealt with the citizens of Weimar. They raped...and they killed...and they ransacked homes."

"They want their revenge..." *Mutti* whispered. "War makes humans act like animals. I heard," she continued in a low voice, "the Americans made the citizens of Weimar tour Buchenwald...not once, but twice."

"Why?"

"They are trying to make the German people..." Mutti's voice broke, "all of us...confront and recall, forever, the atrocities committed by our fathers...by our husbands...by our sons...."

7

As the first flowers sprang through the bloodstained soil of Germany, the Americans arrived in Apolda and made their headquarters just two villas down the avenue.

The wide tree lined street, normally quiet except for the sound of sirens, that now and then stretched like a tight-wire through town announcing nearby bombers, was filled with the hum of American jeeps and army trucks.

I pressed my face between my hands holding the wrought iron bars of the ornate fence that stretched around the villa, now the designated American headquarters, and watched the goings on in the front yard.

Dapper khaki-clad GIs hurried in and out of the building. Off to the side stood a GI facing a single long line of German boys and girls. Not dapper at all, his face was blotchy red and his stomach protruded over his belt.

I clamped my jaw tight and watched as he lifted one child after the other into his arms releasing them only after receiving a kiss. The reward, each time, was a stick of gum. I didn't know what possessed those boys and girls, none of whom I recognized, to relinquish their pride for a stick of gum. "You must always be proud," *Mutti* said more than once. "You have Prussian blood running through your veins. Prussians are good people... honest, hard working, and proud."

Sorrow squeezed my heart watching those boys and girls. I didn't have much, but at least, I still had my pride. I let go of the iron fence bars, and started for home, when I heard someone whistle a tune, velvety with sadness. Transfixed by the melody, I stopped and listened. The melody was similar to a song I heard before, a song about a soldier. Like wind on a river, the words rippled through my mind.

~ * ~

Es steht ein Soldat am Wolgastrand, a soldier stands at *Wolga's* shore... *hält Wache für sein Vaterland*, holds watch for his fatherland...that was it. My father played the song on his harmonica. Sometimes he would remove the harmonica from his lips and sing the words of the refrain...*Hast Du dort oben vergessen auch mich*, have you, up there, forgotten me? *Es sehnt doch mein Herz auch nach Liebe sich*, my heart, after all, also longs for love. *Du hast im Himmel viel Engel bei Dir*, you have in heaven angels galore. *Schick doch einen davon auch zu mir*, won't you send one of them down to me.

~ * ~

Wondering what foreign shore *Vati* was near, and if I would ever see him again, I let my eyes roam the yard in search of the whistler. A cigarette in one side of his mouth with the sunshine breaking across his face through a cloud of smoke, and his arms folded across his chest, the GI leaned against the door of his jeep parked in the circular pebble driveway. His hair was curly and cropped, and his dark olive skin added to his attractiveness. He stopped whistling when I caught his eye, and he winked. I didn't know what to make of this. Perhaps he was ill, I thought. Why else would his eye have a twitch like that? I gave him a narrowed measuring look, contemplating what might be ailing him when, with an easy smile at the corners of his mouth, he winked again. Still I did not know what to make of it, so I blinked at him. This made his smile wider, the kind that forced one to smile back, and with a wave of his hand, he invited me to come into the yard.

When I saw him reach into his jeep and pull out a Hershey bar, I hastened my step and grabbed it quick before he could change his mind, or before I remembered I had pride. What did I care about pride? All I wanted was not to be so hungry any more. I did a curtsy, like the polite child I was, and ran out the yard with my treasure in hand.

My stomach growled. Go ahead…taste the rich creamy chocolate, it appealed. I persevered and hurried home. I needed to share it with Rosel, who was coughing all the time now, and getting weaker and weaker.

8

"I don't want you to beg." Mutti spoke in a low voice reserved for ambivalent things. On one hand she looked content watching us savor the delectable chocolate, declining even a taste of it. "*Nein nein*, I never liked chocolate," she claimed when Rosel offered a piece. On the other hand, she disapproved of the way I acquired it. This, however, was not the reason she refused a bite. I was sure, she just wanted us to have it all.

"I didn't beg," I insisted. "I just did this, see?" I batted one eyelid up and down, to show her how it was done.

Mutti shook her head disapprovingly. When a knock interrupted her reprimand, she turned on her heel and walked to the door.

"Bienchen…but how…but when…?" clutching my cousin's hand, she pulled her inside.

"I have a folding bed…." The lady of the villa, who escorted my cousin to us, hesitated in the doorway. "You'll have to help me bring it up." With a smile, *Mutti* thanked and dismissed her, then closed the door turning her full attention to Bienchen.

"Bienchen…how… when…where…?" Her voice cracked with excitement.

Bienchen, dropping her bag by her side, just stood there and smiled. Two dimples appeared, as if her cheeks had been squeezed too many times by caring fingers. Her nose was speckled with freckles, and her eyes, darting from *Mutti* to Rosel to me, were edged with featherlike laugh lines.

"Do you like chocolate?" I asked, hoping perhaps like *Mutti*, she also wasn't fond of it.

"*Ja,* of course." Bienchen came toward me, even her walk had a sunny exuberance. "Where on earth, did you get this from?"

Instead of an answer, I gave her a wide-eyed innocent look and held out my last morsel of chocolate, feeling regret and pleasure all jumbled together.

~ * ~

Every day I went back to the American headquarters and stood by the fence until I spied the handsome GI, the one with the curly hair. Every day when our eyes met, he winked first and then I winked back. And that is how I got my Hershey bar, every day, which I always brought home and shared, except with *Mutti* who still maintained she didn't like chocolate, but who, halfheartedly, accepted the fact that winking was not begging and so perhaps, it was okay after all to accept the chocolate from the American.

~ * ~

Totally at ease in her new cramped surroundings, Bienchen, several years older than my sister, had a competent way of handling herself, and so *Mutti* left her in charge while she went back home to

auf Wiedersehen

Görlitz hoping to retrieve some of our belongings. "Anything of value can be used to trade in for food," she explained before leaving.

~ * ~

Klaus and the rest of the group were setting up the puppet theater by the gazebo. I was standing by the window and looked outside when Bienchen's voice bounced to my spot. "Let's make potato salad for supper today."

"I have to go." I turned away from the window, and looked with regret at my cousin. "I can't stay and help. We are rehearsing for the show. Can I go?"

"*Ja, ja*...you can go...Rosel will help me peel the potatoes." Her melodic voice rang over the bubbling and fizzling sound coming from the two-burner plate, and my sister obliged with a quick nod. Bienchen took charge with cheerful assurance in *Mutti's* absence. "You go and play. When you come back, we'll have a most luscious potato salad." She smacked her lips in emphasis.

~ * ~

After an hour or so of practice with my friends, I announced, "I have to run." The play was coming along fine.

"Why do you have to leave already?" Klaus asked, crossing his arms over his chest.

"I have to go somewhere," I said, turning away from his questioning gaze.

"You have to go where?" Klaus narrowed his eyes.

I didn't want him to know I was going to see my GI, and so I just grumbled a reply.

"I think next Sunday we should have the show, Sunday afternoon at two," Klaus announced. Everyone agreed with an exuberant *ja*.

"I know my part well," I assured Klaus and the rest of them, who stood scattered behind him. "Really, I say my lines in my head each night." With urgency in my voice, I added, "I do have to go." Off I ran.

Gasping for air, I arrived at the American headquarters and looked through the fence for my GI. The yard was empty.

~ * ~

"Who are you looking for?" His head tilted, and holding on to the suspenders of his Lederhosen, Klaus ambled toward me, followed by the rest of our theater troupe. They lined up along the fence, and looked through the iron bars.

"Where did the Americans go?" I asked as if they should know.

No one knew except the littlest one who shifted his weight from foot to foot, and raised his hand as if in school again. "I know…I know…"

Now everyone left their spot by the fence and circled him.

"You do not." His bigger brother pulled the little one's cap over his eyes.

"I do so." Squinting from underneath the lip of the cap, the little one seemed very pleased with him-self. "They're rounding up all the SS." He took off his cap and repositioned it properly on his head.

"They are not."

"They are so," the little one spluttered through his brother's cupped hand on his mouth. "I heard *Grossmutter* say so."

"What did she say?" Klaus asked, removing the brother's hand from the little one's mouth.

"She said she saw the Americans come next door."

"And…?" Klaus urged him on with a wave of his hand.

"They jumped off the truck…they aimed their rifles like so…" He raised his arms and pointed an imaginary rifle at Klaus. "They circled the house."

"Then what happened?" one of the bigger girls asked.

"Then they brought *Herr* Schoene out and made him go into the truck."

"Where did they take him?" the same girl asked.

"*Grossmutter* wasn't sure at first." The little one tapped his chin with his index finger. "She ran up to the attic, and she saw the truck drive out of town."

"Out of town where?" The big brother elbowed the little one in the side of the ribs to make him go on.

"They stopped at an old barn."

"And?" The group became restless wanting to hear and beginning to fear the outcome of *Herr* Schoene.

"Don't make it so suspenseful. Say already what happened," Klaus urged.

"The Americans made all of them get off the truck. They herded them into the barn. They closed all the doors. They fired through the walls." The little one took a deep breath as if a load lifted off his chest. "That's what I heard *Grossmutter* say."

~ * ~

Why do people have to kill people, I wondered walking home without my Hershey bar.

Bienchen, sensing the sadness in my heart, and seeing I had no chocolate, hugged me and said, "Wait till you taste our potato salad." I had to admit, it was the best potato salad I ever had.

"You should have seen it." *Mutti* swallowed hard. She returned from Görlitz empty-handed and grief-stricken. "They wouldn't even let me come in. From the door I saw enough. The place was a mess."

It seems total strangers now occupied our home in Görlitz and, having taken possession of all our things, refused her entry. In need to vent her frustration, *Mutti* walked around the room aimlessly until Rosel started to cough.

"Where is the cod liver oil?" *Mutti* asked, stopping in front of the cabinet and pushing aside some bottles. Cod liver oil, one of the few things still available, was used for all sorts of ailments, one spoon at a time.

Instead of answering, I pulled my ear, Rosel coughed, and Bienchen fixed her eyes on the floor as if finding it there.

"So, where's the cod liver oil?" Mutti repeated the question.

"Oh…we…" Bienchen began to stammer. "We used it all up to make potato salad."

"You what?" Mutti shook her head disapprovingly, and once again a knock at the door interrupted any further discussion. She turned away from Bienchen and walked to the door. "Hans…?"

9

Hans took a deep breath and adjusted his smile then walked, favoring one leg, into the room. His limp emphasized the power of his thighs below narrow hips. Combing back with his fingertips a mass of raven hair that tumbled down his forehead, his eyes strayed from *Mutti* to Rosel to me, and then rested on Bienchen.

Bienchen, on tiptoes and stretched as tall as a flagpole, wound her arms around her brother's neck. Tears mingled with the sunshine in her eyes, and so it was with me. Through rainbow colors I saw my cousin. It was love at first sight.

His presence was compelling. He towered over us womenfolk in the tiny room, and his massive shoulders strained against the seams of his dust-encrusted jacket.

"Here, let me help you." *Mutti* peeled off his jacket, down his muscular arms.

His profile was rugged and somber with lines around his eyes and mouth, muting his boyishness. Captivated by his handsome good looks, my feelings bubbled to explosion level, and I couldn't wait to tell Klaus, my best friend, all about Hans.

~ * ~

"You can't fall in love with your cousin," Klaus grabbed my shoulder with one hand, and squeezing his eyes narrow brought them close to mine.

"Why not?" I asked.

"Because Hitler is a stickler for things like that."

"What do you mean?"

"Listen…a while back…my cousin Hildegard…she fell in love with her cousin Helmuth. They were just like Juliet and Romeo. Their names, of course, were different."

"Who are Juliet and Romeo?" I was getting confused.

"Never mind…I'll explain that another time."

"So what about Hildegard and Helmuth?"

"They were so in love." Klaus looked into space as if seeing them there.

"They couldn't marry. Hitler didn't allow it, even though his own mother and father were closely related. So closely related, in fact, they had to get papers from the Vatican before they married, Hitler's parents I mean. Can you imagine that?"

"I can't imagine that."

"Did you know Hitler was an altar boy?"

Klaus was a few years older than me and knew so much more. He was my sister's age. Maybe Rosel knew all this too, but she never talked to me about such things. I was really lucky to have a friend like Klaus who taught me so much. If we had school, which we did not, because of the shortage of fuel, I most likely would have known all this too, but things being as they were, I made my ears pay attention. "Now on the other hand," Klaus continued, "if you were a Muslim, you could marry your cousin, did you know that?" Klaus looked at me importantly.

"I didn't know that. How do you know all this?"

"I heard my mom and aunt talk when Hildgard and Helmuth…anyway…Muslims prefer cousins to strangers when they fall in love."

"Makes good sense to me," I said giving my words a decisive nod.

"Who are Muslims?"

"They're people living somewhere in the desert," he explained. "They don't believe in Christ…they believe in Buddha…no not Buddha, Mohammed I think…"

"So what happened to Hildegard and Helmuth?" I interrupted being more interested in my own possible fate than in those people living somewhere in the desert.

"Hildegard slit her wrists and bled to death…I don't know what became of Helmuth." Klaus kicked the dirt hard and bit his lip. A drop of blood fell on his dusty shoe.

~ * ~

I hated that Hitler. No wonder *Mutti* refused to say "*Heil* Hitler." Maybe, she too loved a cousin more than *Vati*. Maybe then I wouldn't be, or maybe then I'd be different, or maybe…

~ * ~

"*Na* Du…" Hans tapped me on my head. His gentle rough hand brought me back from my thoughts and sent a surge of happiness into the cellar of my soul, and all I could do was grin.

10

"You ate all of them?" *Mutti* asked her voice edged with skepticism.

Bienchen quickly came to her brother's defense. "I told him he could have my share," she said, stepping next to him.

"Mine too…" Rosel stepped to the other side of Hans, and made her eyes smile up at him.

I pushed myself between my sister and Hans, and making my eyes smile at him even more, I lied, "I told him he could have my portion too."

Hanging his head, like a puppy caught eating his master's shoe, Hans stumbled over his words, "I…I…didn't know that was all there was."

Hans started lunch without us. Once he started to eat, he couldn't stop, and wolfed down the whole pot of boiled potatoes, all five pounds of them.

"All of them…?" *Mutti* turned around and looked directly at Hans. "*Nein*, it can't be."

Hans shrugged his shoulders in submission.

auf Wiedersehen

Mutti shook her head from side to side, and walked to the cabinet. She took out the bread, sliced off a few pieces, and placed a wedge on each of our empty plates.

"Once I work on the *Bauernhof*, I'll make sure you'll have enough to eat." Hans was trying to ease his guilt, I could tell. "I'll bring you eggs, and bacon, and…"

"I know, I know." *Mutti* gave him a forgiving smile. She'd found a place for Hans on a farm in a nearby village. For food and bed, he would work in the fields. Although he still limped, his leg was well enough to start, and he was to leave in the morning.

"I'll work hard…you'll see…"

"*Ja ja*, Hans." Mutti walked up to him and, circling her arms around him from behind, she rested her head sideways on his young strong back. She looked tired, but managed a smile.

~ * ~

I had nothing to smile about. The men in my life were always saying *auf Wiedersehen*, Günter, the American GI, and now Hans. *Vati* had been gone for so long, he no longer was on the list. Thank God I still had Klaus…

~ * ~

Klaus, his eyes like the clear blue sky, was waiting in the garden. Today was the day of our puppet show.

"Hey, Klaus," I shouted and waved, pushing through the crowd that ambled toward the gazebo. He and the other kids were setting up the playhouse.

Sunbeams slanted through the trees and served as stage-light. The birds filled in as our orchestra.

"It's about time you got here." Klaus looked at me reproachfully. Excitement tinted his cheeks a shade of red. I took my place next to him behind the playhouse, and together we went over each puppet and laid them down in the order they would perform, just as we'd done a hundred times before during our practice sessions.

Anticipation mounted as more and more people arrived. They took their weight off their feet in the makeshift rows of seats, and exchanged pleasantries.

"*Wie geht es Frau* Schmidt? How are you Mrs. Schmidt?"

"*Es geht mir recht gut.* I am quite well. How are you?"

"*Na ja…*Oh yes…"

Even the owners of the villa came and, with a nod of their heads, thanked the older girl from our troupe, who ushered them to their row. The lady of the villa did not purse her lips, did not draw her eyebrows together, as she took a seat with her husband on the makeshift benches. Instead, a smile played around her lips in happiness. Everyone came to have a good time. Forgotten was the animosity between resident and refugee. Forgotten was the fear of the advancing Red Army. Forgotten was all horror of war, if only for a little while. Never before was the garden more magical. The show was about to begin.

~ * ~

The curtain parted. Klaus manipulated the king, I the queen, and the older girl the jester. The other kids vocalized the imaginary characters in the king's courtyard whenever it was necessary.

auf Wiedersehen

To our delight, everything went along fine and the audience sat awestruck throughout the first and second act, each time applauding with gusto.

"You must die," the king shrieked toward the end of the third act. A hush fell over the audience as tension rose. "Take him to the dungeon." Suddenly, the sound of footsteps on crunching pebbles coming nearer and nearer interrupted the spell. Time stood still as everyone turned to look.

With purposeful intent in her walk, Klaus' mother rushed toward our troupe. Panting, she yanked her son up by the collar of his shirt yelling, "I told you to get the puppets back. I told you we need them for firewood." Poor Klaus. He looked more like a puppet than puppeteer as his mother dragged him out from behind the playhouse.

The passion of that final show stayed with us for a very long time. Long after the last puppet warmed Klaus' soup. Long after Hitler, who had been hiding in a Berlin bunker, put a gun to his head. Long after the Americans left, and the Russians marched in. Long after the Germans laid down their arms, and searched in the ashes for something or someone.

We children still met each day in the garden, downhearted and lost. I missed Klaus who didn't come back after the incident.

Then one day, a day in early August, when the sky was full of gray haze adding to our gloom, the villa's lady came trotting down the garden path carrying a huge box. In her usual haughty way, she dropped the box at our feet. Catching her breath, and pointing to the gazebo, she said, "There is your stage…and here," she pointed down at the box, "here are your costumes."

For a moment we remained still, but then the littlest one in our group stepped forward and took a look. "Prima," he exclaimed.

Whooping and hollering, we pulled out gowns, and wraps, and elbow- length gloves, and even a tuxedo and a top hat.

"We have no more use for them," the lady of the villa said, stepping back and pausing for a moment reflectively. Then clearing her throat and in half an octave higher she continued, "Oh, and I talked to Klaus' mother. He'll be here any minute. I presume you'll need him in your next show. She clapped her hands together then, and urged, "*Kommt, macht schnell*...start practicing...the show must go on."

11

Like tidal waves, the golden rye danced in the mild August wind, and white clouds scudded playfully across the blue sky. We were walking home along a country road, from a day's work on a farm in a nearby village. It was not the farm where Hans was, but one nearer to Apolda, one within walking distance. Rosel and I accompanied *Mutti*, who helped the farmer's wife in the house, in the barn, in the garden, hoping to bring home some fat, or potatoes, or cabbage. The farmer's wife, while preparing a pig roast, potato dumplings, and red cabbage, felt the bread and *schmaltz* she provided for all three of us for lunch was enough payment for one day's labor.

"Come back next week," she said. "I'll have more work for you."

Anger glittered in *Mutti's* eyes, relentless and vivid, as she walked with stalking intent between Rosel and me. The road was lined with trees on each side bordering the rye field, trees laden with almost ripe apples.

Suddenly, *Mutti* stopped, and, shading her eyes with one hand, she let her gaze roam down the dirt country road stretching out before us to where it met the sky. No one in sight, she scrambled up the embankment on all fours. She gathered her apron ends, making a pouch, and reached for the nearest branch. She twisted an apple, snapping it off the stem, and then dropped it into her apron pouch.

"*Ja ja*, it's okay." She nodded with a smile, making the anger in her eyes go away. "Come…help me pick."

We hesitated, Rosel and I, wondering what possessed our mother to steal. "Prussians don't beg, they work for their food," she told us often enough. "They never ever steal, *nein*."

"Hitler had these trees planted for the German people." She nodded her head as if to convince herself of what her tone of voice seemed to imply, Hitler did something nice.

Through Mutti's eyes, I always saw the *Führer*, no longer alive, as a monster. Could it be then she had a change of mind? Or was she just too tired to care anymore? It was very confusing to me.

Pondering this, I climbed up the embankment and picked an apple for her. I was about to pick another, when the sea of rye divided as if Moses waved his rod over it, and the farmer wife's came lumbering through, flailing both arms.

"Halt. You are stealing my apples," she yelled. Panting and snorting like a bull facing his matador, she yanked at *Mutti's* apron.

Mutti held on tight. "They're not your apples," she tried to reason. "These trees are along the road and not in your field."

"You are a thief." The farmer's wife spat, ignoring Mutti's words. She yanked harder at the apron, and still *Mutti* held on tight.

We stood rooted to our spot, Rosel and I, very much like the apple trees, watching in stark silence, the two women fighting it out.

"Give me back my apples, you dirty refugee thief," the farmer's wife yelled.

"They're not yours," Mutti yelled back and trying to grab the farmer wife's hair, she added between clenched teeth, "*dumme Schlampe*." And still she held on to her apples.

auf Wiedersehen

In the distance a cloud of dust appeared. Getting thicker and thicker, it came closer and closer.

It was a Russian convoy. An officer, tall and wide shouldered, stood on the leading Panzer, legs widespread and hands on slender hips. He raised his arm and brought the convoy to a stop. For a minute the Russian observed, from atop his tank, the two women who were so engrossed in their tug of war, that they ignored their fear of the intruders.

The Russian officer jumped down and approaching them asked in broken German words, "*Was ist hier los?*"

Rosel trembled and coughed. "Is he going to rape us?" she asked. Word had gotten around from whispering mouth to whispering mouth, the Russian Army left a trail of blood and raped women along the way as they entered each town on their westward drive. Although I did not know what rape was, I knew it was bad. *Mutti*, without any details, instructed us what to do, just in case.

"Kick real hard between the legs, and then run as fast as you can." Those were her exact words. "That is where it will hurt most and give you a chance to get away."

I knew, of course, what was between a man's legs. I peeked once when Günter peed, outside, a long time ago. He made his little waterspout go high and far, aiming for the fence. I had been impressed. A hard kick, no doubt, could be quite damaging to that little spout, ruining for life, its aim.

Although this Russian, unlike the others I saw before in town, did not look menacing at all, I practiced in my mind to kick hard where it hurt most. While he winced in pain, in my mind that is, the two women ended, at last, their tug of war.

"She stole my apples." The farmer's wife foamed at the mouth like a bull that had seen better days. She waved her arms from *Mutti*, to the tree, to the apples in *Mutti's* apron.

The Russian officer pushed back his cap and scratched his head, then shook it in bewilderment.

"These trees are along the road and belong to everyone," *Mutti* tried to make him see by pointing to the road and to the trees.

"She lies," the farmer's wife cried. Indicating the barn and house beyond the field with a jerk of her double chin. "You can see," she said, "they are mine."

The Russian officer raised a brow, then walked up to *Mutti* and with one yank made the apples roll to the ground. Turning to the still blustering farmer's wife, his mouth twisted wryly. "Your apples."

He was halfway down the embankment when a sob escaped *Mutti's* lips. She let her head drop to her heart and stood there in a pose of weariness, her last shreds of pride falling away.

The Russian officer stopped midway, turned around, and in a few strides was next to *Mutti*. Gathering her apron ends in one hand and pulling her along, he reached up the tree with the other hand, and picking only the biggest and ripest apples, he filled up her pouch once again.

"Here…your apples," he said. A smile played on his lips.

Then turning to the farmer's wife, he pointed across the field and yelled "*Geh heim…schnell.*"

The farmer's wife gasped and fled through the rye. The Russian officer bobbed down the embankment then, and leapt up on his tank. He raised his arm and with a forward wave, his tank began to sputter to life and the convoy moved on.

He turned back, once, and glanced at me. I made my eye blink and gave him the American wink. He did not wink back, he just grinned.

"Mutti…all Russians aren't bad, are they?" Rosel asked as we headed home into the sunset.

"No…" *Mutti* smiled. "Not all Russians are bad. Some are very good."

And the wind sang and made the rye dance, like tidal waves coming in, swoosh, swoosh, swoosh.

12

"We're going to America." The excitement unleashed in *Mutti's* voice matched the gleam in her eyes, as she danced into the room. She waved an envelope in her hand, an envelope edged in blue and red signifying it came by air, it came from far away.

"It's from America, it's from my friend Paul Westendorf." She walked to the table, pulled out the chair, and sat down. Sunshine streaked across her face as she opened the envelope and began to read. Her eyes skipped down the lines from left to right, and when half way down the page, she stopped.

"He says," she turned her head, half facing Bienchen, Rosel, and me, who had come up behind her, trying to catch a glimpse. " He says, it came as quite a surprise and it warmed his heart to hear from me after all these years." *Mutti* sat back in her chair and dropped her hands, holding the letter, in her lap, "He is glad to hear from me, imagine that."

"Go on…go on…" Bienchen squeezed her shoulder.

"He never married, he says. He remained single all his life." *Mutti's* eyes flew down the page and then she paused once more. "He lives alone in a house by a river, and he owns a car, imagine that."

"Wow…" Bienchen smiled and her dimples came alive. "He must be a millionaire."

"In America, many people own a car," Rosel informed her. "You don't have to be a millionaire."

"How do you know?" I was curious.

"A car, in America, costs less than two thousand Mark, that's how. Not a million."

"How do you know that?" I asked again.

"You would know too," she said. "If sometimes you would read a book instead of always playing in the garden."

"Girls…girls…" *Mutti* interrupted our banter.

"Listen to this. He says he sent a care package for us, with food and clothes. Imagine that."

"Is he your boyfriend?" I asked. Seeing the glow in *Mutti's* eyes I wondered if maybe…

"*Aber nein…*" Mutti laughed.

I pressed on. "So why is he writing to you and sending us packages?"

"Because he's a good man. We met long ago, when we were both very young."

"Where did you meet?" I was intrigued.

"We met in the Salvation Army." She lowered her voice as if to assure that no one else could hear.

"You were in the army? You were a soldier? You fought in the war?" I was amazed.

"Sort of…but it's a different kind of army and it fights a different kind of war."

"What do you mean?" My curiosity was beginning to boil over.

"The Salvation Army is a Christian organization. It's an army of compassion, fighting for human dignity and hope."

"I didn't know you did that." Rosel looked at Mutti with renewed admiration. "When did you start to do that?"

"Your mother was still very young." Bienchen's eyes were full of merriment. "Is it not so?" She turned to *Mutti*, and then turning to us, she asked, "and do you know why she joined?"

Rosel and I looked at Bienchen, eager to hear that our mother had blazed with passion to save mankind, but instead Bienchen said, "Because at Eastertime the Salvation Army, in our part of Königsberg, gave out the biggest chocolate eggs."

It's true." Mutti laughed to cover her embarrassment. They did give out the most fantastic chocolate eggs I could not resist."

"I thought you didn't like chocolate?" With hands on hips, Rosel stepped around the table and faced Mutti.

Ignoring Rosel, Mutti went on. "As I grew up, the Salvation Army sent me to school in Berlin, where I trained to become a child care mentor."

"What's that?" I asked, anticipation once more rising.

"It's someone who…" she sighed, and sadness shadowed her face. "It's someone who works with children. I was their teacher, and I was their guardian, so to speak. Sometimes, accompanied by the *Polizei*, I had to remove a child from an alcoholic mother, an abusive father, or the like. It was the hardest thing in my life I ever had to do."

"The Salvation Army tried to save the riffraff of society, too," Bienchen threw in. Dressed in their uniforms, they'd march in step to their band's music, oom-pah, oom-pah, oom-pah-pah." Bienchen paraded around the room pretending to play a trombone. "They brought their music and word of God into the worst sections of town, where ladies of ill repute and sailors sneered and spit at them."

"*Ja ja*, it's true. We were laughed at all the time." Mutti lowered her lids, so no one could look into her eyes. "That's why I don't like to talk about it. How do you know all this, Bienchen?" Before receiving an answer, she nodded her head. "Of course...my sister...your mother...told you."

I got the picture Bienchen's mother, Lieschen, the spoiled one, the snow-white look-alike, had not approved of her sister's involvement with the Salvation Army.

Bienchen hugged *Mutti's* shoulders then, and in a voice full of apology she said, "I'm sorry, I didn't mean to hurt your feelings. It's just..." *Mutti* swiveled around in her chair to face Bienchen. "*Schon gut.* You should know the Salvation Army does much good, even today, and they have very fine musicians in their bands."

"*Ja, ja...*" Bienchen, sorry to have caused hurt feelings, readily agreed.

"I don't know why people always poked fun at us." *Mutti* reflected on this for a moment. "It's where I met Martin, your uncle," she turned from Bienchen to Rosel and me. "Your father was playing the lead trumpet in the Salvation Army Kapelle when we first met."

"Did your friend play in the band too?" I asked.

"*Nein, nein,* Paul was active in other ways. Then he went to America and no one heard from him again. Until today, that is."

"Now he's a millionaire with a mansion by the river and a Cadillac," Bienchen exclaimed with awe."

"*Mutti...*" Rosel coughed. "Does *Vati* know about him, about your rich friend, I mean?"

"*Nein,* they never met. Paul left before your father joined. We'll have to tell him when he comes home from the war."

"We're no longer at war, why isn't *Vati* here yet?" I wanted to know.

"He doesn't know where we are. He has to find us first."

"How did your friend know where we are, I asked?"

"I wrote his sister in the Saar Gebiet, and asked her for his address, and then I wrote to him. That's how he knows where we are."

"Did your friend say we could come to America?" Rosel asked.

"*Nein*, not yet. He will, I think. As for your father, he'll find us through the Red Cross. Now go." She shooed us away with a wave of her hand. "All of you…enough with the questions already. No more talk about the Salvation Army, do you hear? Promise."

So we promised, a promise I was to keep for a very long time, until after *Mutti* died.

13

"Guess what? " I shouted as soon as I saw Klaus in the garden early the next day. "We're going to America."

"When?" Klaus kicked the pebbles and made them fly high into the air.

"I don't know…as soon as my father returns, I guess. As soon as my mother's friend says it's okay, I guess. As soon as we get tickets, I guess."

"Do you have a visa?" Klaus asked.

"What's that?"

"I don't know, but they won't let you in unless you have one."

Klaus' know-it-all attitude was beginning to get on my nerves.

"That's why so many Jews had to die."

"Had to what?"

"They couldn't get visas to go to America. America closed their doors and claimed their quota was filled. it wasn't even filled, at all, yet."

"What's a quota?"

"It's like a measurement of how many people of a certain race, or occupation, or age, can enter a country."

"How do you know all this?"

"I know because my cousin Josef, he's older than me, he has a friend who has an uncle who was married to this really beautiful lady. Her grandmother was Jewish...maybe it was her mother...I'm not sure if it was her mother or grandmother. Anyway, they tried to go to America, Josef's friend's uncle and his wife that is, but they were told the quota was filled. That was, of course, before they took Josef's friend's uncle's wife away."

I listened attentively and said, "I didn't realize it was so complicated." I bit my lip. "Maybe then they won't want us either."

"*Ja*, they'll want you. They just don't want the Jews. Nobody wants the Jews. That's why Hitler ordered..."

"Hitler ordered what?"

"Never mind. I don't want to talk about it anymore. Besides, I only know what my cousin Josef told me, and he's an idiot."

"Tell me what he said," I begged. "I heard my mother and the lady of the villa talk...a while ago...something about a concentration camp ...atrocities... what does it all mean?"

Klaus pushed his lip forward in thought, but then he shook his head from side to side. "Come on...forget about it...we have to rehearse for the next play. We have decided, you are Juliet and I am Romeo."

"Who decided?" I shifted my weight from foot to foot. "When did you decide that?"

"Yesterday when you weren't here. Come on...we have to practice. Stand up there." He pointed to the gazebo. "Go up there, and look down at me affectionately. Then, try and moan with ecstasy, and say, Romeo, oh Romeo."

"What's ecstasy?" I wanted to know.

"It's like...it's like...well you know, it's like romantic, it's like happy...It's like you are in seventh heaven."

auf Wiedersehen

"I didn't know there are seven heavens. What's so special about the seventh one?"

"Oh never mind," Klaus said. His voice was bursting with impatience. So I climbed the stairs and, grasping the railing with my two hands, I did a long slow slide with my eyes down to my Romeo.

My Romeo in *Lederhosen*, his knees skinned, his hair in a clash with the wind, raised the shutters of his blue eyes and looked at me adoringly.

"A-a- h Romeo, oh Romeo…" I sighed, pretending to be in seventh heaven, happy like.

"No, no. That's too *schmaltzig*." Klaus raised his hand in protest. "Try and sound romantic, not *schmaltzig*."

I exhaled a big sigh. "I don't know if I can do this."

"Yes, yes, you can do it. Try again, and when you look at me, think I am your cousin Hans, you know…the one you adore."

"A-a-h Romeo, oh Romeo…"

"Cut." A stranger emerged from behind a tree. Amusement lurked in his eyes as he, with the grace of a wild cat, approached.

Klaus turned to him. "Who are you?"

"My name, young man," the stranger held out his hand, "is Martin Holder." As Klaus grasped the extended hand, the stranger's eyes moved up into mine and he said, "I am your Juliet's father."

While Klaus pumped the stranger's hand, I stood there, with my hands still gripping the railing, with my breath caught in my lungs, and with my eyes widening in astonishment.

"*Vati…?*"

14

"Anna?" His gaze focused on *Mutti* who was, sitting, curled over the table in her usual posture of concentration, her glasses idle, at arm's length, her nose almost touching her writing pad.

She jumped at the sound of his voice and turned to look at the stranger, my father, still holding my hand, who paused just inside the door. With a sigh louder than the surf of the Baltic Sea, she whispered, "Martin… when…how…?"

I let go of my father's hand and joined Rosel and Bienchen who stood, their backs to the window and mouths wide open, gaping at the visitor.

"How did you get here?" *Mutti* asked faintly, drawing a step toward *Vati* who waited by the door with his hand outstretched, frozen in a triumphant tableau.

Warmth surged through me as the scene unfolded with hugs, and kisses, and questions galore.

auf Wiedersehen

~ * ~

Mutti pulled out the fine linen tablecloth – the one with the pretty red, yellow, and blue, hand stitched flowers, the one that her mother, our *Oma* Machein, the scientific miracle who lived without a stomach for quite a while, gave her on her wedding day. She stepped away from the table to see if the ends hanging over each side were even, and when she saw they were not, she pulled on one end until they were perfectly in line. Rosel positioned two candlesticks with only stubs, and struck a match to light them up. Our shadows, backlit by the flickering candlelight, danced merrily on the far wall, while over potatoes and salt, we chatted, we laughed, and wept, and we asked and answered questions, until, exhausted, *Vati* said, "We'll talk more tomorrow. I'm really tired. *Gute Nacht.*"

~ * ~

"First…we get Hans." All eyes watched *Vati* with interest, as he strutted around the small room, with his hands clasped behind his back, revealing his plans to us. "Then we all go to Osterode." A compact man, devastatingly handsome, he moved with the demeanor of a peacock in command of the situation.

"Where is Osterode?" *Mutti* asked, her brows knitted in a frown.

"Osterode is in the Harz Mountains. It's a beautiful medieval town surrounded by forests and hills." *Vati* stopped prancing, and turned to look directly at *Mutti* with his extraordinary laughing eyes, the color of sea green, ringed with gold. "You'll like it there."

"How do you propose we get there?" The intensity in Mutti's lowered voice matched the sound of an alarm going off in my mind.

"Not the way you came, I hope. Perhaps you'll have a chauffeur waiting to drive us across the border."

Mutti's unkind remark prompted a chuckle from Bienchen who sat next to Rosel and me on the bed, listening intently.

Osterode was in the American Zone. Apolda was in the Russian Zone. *Vati,* under the cover of darkness, had sneaked across the border at night dodging bullets and barking dogs.

He gave an impatient shrug. "Would you rather we stay here?" He gestured in a sweeping motion with one arm across the tiny room. Here, where we have to walk down the hall and stand in line to pee? We have two rooms waiting for us in Osterode. There's a job waiting for me in an ironworks plant."

"I don't want to go." Rosel coughed, and coughed, and coughed.

Vati watched and listened, his laughing eyes turned sad, until at last the coughing spell was over.

"There is your answer," *Vati* walked over to *Mutti* and, pulling his shoulders back to stand as tall as *Mutti,* he lifted her chin between his thumb and forefinger, holding her grave sapphire eyes captive in his. With the fingertips of his free hand he combed back a strand of hair, that freed itself from the chignon on the back of her head, and said, "We have to go. In the American Zone, our child will get the right treatment. She will get well. I promise you."

All eyes now gravitated to *Mutti* who stepped out of his reach and walked to the window. She looked outside, not saying a word. She craned her neck and waved to someone down in the garden, and after another minute or so, she turned around.

"All right," she said, that old familiar glimmer of strength returned to her eyes as she spoke. "We'll go, but we'll go in daylight…we'll take our chances…we'll go through the checkpoints."

auf Wiedersehen

"The Russians will not let us through," *Vati* tried to protest. Knowing his wife's Prussian determination, he conceded and said, while twisting his gold wedding band around and around, "we'll have to try and buy our way across."

"Listen," *Mutti* sat down in the chair by the table, and folding her hands, as if in prayer, she said, "The Russians have a good heart where children are concerned. We'll have to practice with the girls, crying."

"Oh good," Bienchen said, getting up from the bed. "I'm not a child, and so I don't have to cry. I'd rather laugh, anyway." She walked to the cabinet, and pulled out some plates. "Why don't we have breakfast? Isn't anyone hungry?"

Rosel hugged her knees to herself. I could see her misgivings increase by the minute.

"Russians can't bear to see a child cry," *Mutti* continued. "You girls will have to practice to cry on demand." She looked directly at me. "If we get to a checkpoint, and the Russians won't let us through, I'll give you a signal like this," she attempted to do the American wink by batting her right eyelid, up and down, in a twitch.

"Too obvious..." *Vati* interrupted. "Just tap your nose, like this." He held his elbow in one hand, resting his chin on his thumb, and while his eyes roamed from ceiling to floor in a circular motion, he tapped his nose with the index finger.

Disconcerted, I crossed my arms and looked away. *This was getting ridiculous*, I thought. *How could anyone cry on demand?* Then it came to me, as if lightning struck me. I was able to act ecstatic for Klaus, when we practiced the Romeo and Juliet scene in the garden. All I had to do, then, was have happy thoughts about Hans. Maybe I could act saddened for *Mutti*, when we crossed the border. Maybe, all I had to do was, have unhappy thoughts. I could pretend that Hans was leaving us...or he was ill…or he was dying…It might work. I could feel my eyes become moist already.

That night, after preparing all day for the crossover to the West where a better life awaited us, while we slept, the world trembled and…

~ * ~

An American, in a B-29, asked himself "My God, what have we done?" In seconds sixty-six thousand people were killed, and sixty-nine thousand more were injured when the Americans dropped the first atomic bomb on Hiroshima. Three days later, thirty-nine thousand people died in a flash, and twenty-five thousand more were injured when the Americans dropped the second atomic bomb on Nagasaki. Japan requested to be permitted to surrender, and World War II, at last, was over.

15

"S-h-h," *Mutti* shushed us, holding her head forward, straining to see as she led us down the darkened hallway, past silent doors, down plush carpeted steps, across the marble entryway, through double carved oak doors.

The villa, with its faded stucco façade surrounded by tall trees, loomed stately in the gray mist of dawn.

We slinked along the entry-walk, and *Vati* very slowly opened the heavy iron-gate leading to the street, so as not to make it creak and wake the villa's lady.

The villa's lady, who looked and acted like royalty nine months before when we first arrived at her doorstep, changed. Her appearance was no longer impeccably groomed, and compassion replaced the aloofness in her face.

"Take this." She handed *Mutti* a bottle of French champagne, and dabbing at her eyes with a handkerchief, she said, "It's the last bottle from our wine cellar. When you reach the West, have a toast on us."

Mutti seized the willowy lady into her arms and said, "Thank you so much, *Gnaedige Frau*. You've been most gracious to us."

I do believe the two women had grown fond of each other. More than once, the lady had been helpful, and it was with her aid *Mutti* found a temporary home for Hans on the Bauernhof.

Hans returned from the farm a week before, bronzed, fuller, and content. The family on the farm had been good to him, and although happy to see us again, he was saddened to leave those kindly people. His sadness, however, could not have been as relentless as the sadness that smoldered within me, ever since the farewell to my Romeo Klaus, and the rest of the garden theater gang.

~ * ~

"Why do you have to go?" The littlest one in the group asked, hopping from foot to foot. "I know…I know…" He raised his hand, waiting for permission to answer his own question.

"I don't know," I intervened, speaking to all, but gazing only at Klaus. Because, my father came for us…because, here, there's not enough room for us…because, I don't know…I wish I didn't have to go."

"Who's going to play Juliet now?" Klaus looked at me, his brows drawing downward in a frown.

I let my eyes roam from friend to friend, from the smallest to the tallest, from the youngest to the oldest. One of the older girls, the one with the long dark curls, would do just fine, I thought, and pointed to her.

"She's too tall." Klaus scratched his head, and turned away. A blush crept into the older girl's cheeks. "I don't want to be Juliet, anyway," she mumbled.

auf Wiedersehen

"I mean..." Klaus turned back and blinked, then focused his eyes full of remorse on the older girl. " I mean... I'm too short...and...I mean..."

"Klaus, my father is not so tall, and it's no problem at all." I made my voice bubbly with belief. "All you have to do is stand tall, like so." I pushed my shoulders back, and stretched my neck long. "Besides, the height is not so important, Klaus..." I relaxed and resumed my normal height once more. "The eyes are much more important. And you have real Romeo eyes...really." I bobbed my head up and down to emphasize my words.

"*Ja, ja*...she's right...*ja, ja*..." the others chimed in, agreeing to the selection of my substitute. The blush on the older girl's face began to fade.

"Still, I wish you didn't have to go." Klaus walked to the gazebo, bent down, and picked up a parcel from the steps. Coming toward me, he held out his hands, gripping the box. "Here...this is for you from all of us. Don't open it until you've reached the West. Promise?"

"I promise." I hugged each one of my friends then, swallowing my sobs, and holding the box close to my heart, I ran upstairs into our room. No one was in.

As soon as the door clicked shut, I tore open the box. Inside the box, cushioned by straw, lay the king, the finest puppet of all. A folded sheet of paper was tucked to the side of him. I pulled it out and read, from the ashes I rise to be with my queen. Always, remember me, your friend Klaus...

~ * ~

I remember Klaus, my childhood friend, and the rest of the garden gang. I recall the sadness of our farewell, like wind on water that comes and goes, sometimes tempestuous and sometimes calm, the sadness an intricate maze.

Caught in a battle between good and evil, we children of the Nazi Generation, children of fathers who sang with zest '*Deutschland, Deutschland über alles*' while doing the devil's work, children of mothers who stood by powerless to stop the evil from raging, children ignorant of other children condemned to gas, played and laughed and formed a strong bond. A bond broken the day we said *auf Wiedersehen*.

16

"*Na Du*." Bent forward from the weight of his knapsack, Hans sidled up to me. "Are you sad you have to leave your friends?" Slowing his pace, he fell in step with me. Suddenly, he clutched my shoulder and made me pause in my walk. "Listen…"

I stopped and listened. The street was deserted at this early hour, and so I looked up at him in question.

"Do you hear the lark sing? She's one of your garden friends, is she not?" Hans smiled down into my eyes.

"*J-a-a*…s-o-o…?" I looked all around in search of the bird. "Do you hear what she sings?"

"Of course," I lied, and marched on. Eager to please him, I threw in, "she sings, good-bye…farewell…so long."

"Unh--u-h." He did not accept my answer, and shaking his head from side to side, he said, "Listen…listen again."

I stopped and listened once more, squeezing my eyes shut to concentrate.

"Hear...? She's not singing good-bye at all." Hans cocked his head up and to the side, as if hearing it all very clear. "She's singing...I'll fly with you wherever you go. I'll be your friend. I'll sing with you."

I smiled at him, the kind of smile that said thank you. Then we walked on, much faster now, for we'd fallen behind. The rest of the family was way ahead. They reached the outskirts of town, and the country road leading out of Apolda to the West. When, at last, Hans and I reached the path, the path that stretched between the dew-wet fields, the dew-wet fields that glowed in the luminous light of the rising sun, I, too, heard the lark sing. *I'll fly with you wherever you go. I'll be your friend. I'll sing with you.*

17

The wind came sliding down over the fields and brought dark billowing clouds obscuring the warm October sun. Unexpected lightning hung to the earth. Although all Germany was on foot, going east or going west, going north or going south, homeward bound or to a new nest, we had not come upon anyone. We walked for hours on the deserted country road when *Vati,* at the head of our group, suddenly stopped and dropping his bags, he pointed to the end of the road. "Look...that's the first checkpoint we'll have to get through."

I squinted and focused my eyes to where the sky touched the road, to where a shape, not much bigger than a puppet yet dark and menacing against flashes of lightning, paced back and forth.

Disciplining his voice to pretend assurance, *Vati* rasped, "the Russians are waiting...the Russians are waiting for us."

"Don't worry, we'll be all right." Mutti flashed us a smile of confidence. "Remember," she tapped the end of her Grecian nose. "If you see me do this, cry as hard as you can."

So we trekked on, slower and slower, anxiety rising, as we neared the checkpoint. *Mutti* and *Vati* in front, Rosel and I between Bienchen and Hans, close behind. A Russian soldier marched back and forth in front of the barricade.

"Halt!" With an abrupt stop, the Russian stood riveted facing us, rifle across his shoulder. "Halt!"

Rosel shivered like tall grass in the wind. Fear, stark and vivid, raged in her eyes. My stomach clenched tight.

Vati approached the Russian with battleship formality, gripping the harmonica in his hand.

Standing there, tall and straight like a towering evergreen, the Russian pulled out a cigarette. He stuck it in between his teeth and struck a match to it. He took a deep drag as though sucking in oxygen, while frowning at us.

Vati extended his arm and offered his harmonica that lay in the palm of his open hand. "For you," he said. Then pointing to us and to beyond the barricade, he spoke a few words in Russian no one understood, including the Russian who raised his eyebrows in question and shrugged.

So *Vati* withdrew his arm and, bringing the harmonica to his lips, he began to play the *Wolgalied*.

The Russian, whose rifle remained across his shoulders, spit out his cigarette and, as if in a trance, began to hum in tune the sad melody. Two other Russian soldiers emerged from the sentry house and joined in, humming in harmony.

When they arrived at the refrain that goes, have you, up there, forgotten me? My heart, after all, also longs for love. You have in heaven angels galore. Wont you send one of them down to me, God surely sent one down to them. For when they finished harmonizing, the Russian soldiers took their turn thumping *Vati* on his back, and after accepting the harmonica, they raised the barricade and waved us on.

auf Wiedersehen

I blew out my cheeks. *That wasn't so bad,* I thought. I wondered why everyone was so afraid of them. Just when I arrived at the conclusion that, indeed, they were a likeable group, I heard one of them shout after us in his heavy Russian accent, "*Hals und Beinbruch.*" *Vati* raised his hand in a gesture of acknowledgement.

"Why do they want us to break our neck and our leg?" I asked. "I thought they liked us."

Everyone chuckled and Hans explained, "It really means Good Luck."

How can break your neck, break your leg, possibly mean "Good Luck."

"It's just…" Hans choked down another chuckle. It's just an old German saying. Have you never heard it before?"

"N-o-o-o. It's not nice," I persisted. "It's stupid."

"*Ja*, you're right." Hans nodded and held out his hand, palm up, and looked at the sky. "It's stupid."

A light rain began to fall. I didn't mind. I loved to walk in the rain. We walked, and walked, and walked, until we reached the next checkpoint.

~ * ~

"*Zurück!*" His Russian's eyes blazed with relentless anger and he ground the word out between his teeth. "*Zurück!*"

Blood pounded in my temples as I watched this slovenly excuse for a human being in a Russian uniform reach for the rifle on his shoulders, and clutch it firmly with both hands in front of his chest.

Vati stepped back. It was *Mutti's* turn to beg for our freedom. She stepped forward and, letting her Prussian pride wash away with the rain, her sapphire eyes smiled down into the soldier's soul.

The slovenly soldier relaxed the grip on his rifle. His eyes clawed at *Mutti*, from her face down her neck, down her breast, down her abdomen to the V of her thighs emphasized through the wet skirt clinging to her skin, down her legs, then back up, pausing for too long on her upper thighs, then up to her hands, to her fingers and to her golden wedding band.

She gave an anxious nod of consent, then slipped off the ring and gave it to him. Gesturing toward the barricade, she raised both arms.

The Russian ignored her request and stepped toward *Vati*, pointing at his wedding band. Vati slipped it off and gave it to him.

Smiling, the Russian weighed and jingled both wedding bands in the palm of his hand. As he walked to the side of the barricade, ready to open it, a second soldier emerged. They exchanged words, and then the second one pointed to our luggage. "Vodka?"

Vati nodded in agreement and opened one of the bags. He reached in between clothes and pulled out the bottle of French Champagne the lady of the villa had given us. "For you," he said, and pointing the bottle to the barricade, he extended his arm in an upward motion.

The second Russian soldier pushed him aside and, grabbing the bottle from him, reached with the other hand for the suitcase, spilling out some of the neatly packed clothes. He reached inside, poking around, and pulled out my puppet, my king.

"*Nein*," I screamed and ran toward him, but *Mutti* held me back. I struggled to get free yelling, "*Nein*, he is mine. You can't have him."

Rosel and Bienchen came to *Mutti*'s aid, and the Russian laughed and slipped his hand inside the puppet's frock.

He made the puppet move his head up and down, and clap his hands. *Vati* collected the mud caked dresses and bunched them back into the suitcase, while my beautiful puppet was bobbing up and down in rhythm to the Russian's gruff voice.

auf Wiedersehen

And then my puppet pointed to the slovenly one and to the barricade. The slovenly one sauntered to the side of the road and opened the barricade. Thus, my king let us pass through, waving *auf Wiedersehen*.

~ * ~

"There should be only one more Russian checkpoint," *Vati* explained in a hoarse whisper. "Then a stretch of no man's land, and then the American checkpoint, the entrance of the American Zone."

Everyone was elated we had made it so far, except me. I was angry with all of them. Why didn't they fight to save my king, I wondered. Even Hans, my hero, stood by silently. If only they hadn't held me back, I would have kicked that stupid Russian where it hurt most, and maybe I would still have my king. The rainfall increased, turning the road into a mud bath.

"Once we reach the West, we'll get you another puppet," *Mutti* promised. Her eyes let me know how sad she was for me.

"I don't ever want another puppet." I replied through stiff lips. "I'll never ever perform in a puppet show again." I kicked at the mud and spoke to no one from then on. My weariness grew heavier with each step as did the downpour.

"We have nothing more to trade." *Mutti* glanced at *Vati* through heavy veils of rain, and after a long pause, she asked, "How will we ever get through the next checkpoint?"

Vati, perpetually the optimistic one, made his eyes smile at her from beneath sopping long lashes and said, "Nothing will hold us back now. Osterode, here we come."

"Maybe we should go to America." I heard *Mutti* say as we pushed on in the heavy downpour.

"America?" *Vati* breathed a sigh of astonishment.

"I mean if things don't turn out so good in Osterode...perhaps..." *Mutti* spoke quickly as if to convince, not only *Vati*, but also herself. I mean perhaps...*ja*, I mean we should go to America."

"How would we get there? No money, no sponsor, no anything." His voice contained an edge of regret.

Mutti began to tell him, loud enough for all of us to hear, about her friend in America, and about her dream of a new life for all of us in a new world.

Spellbound, we were pulled into her flight of the imagination and found ourselves, in thought that is, with the good friend in the big mansion by the river, and taking a drive in the Cadillac across the American countryside. Before we knew it, we approached the last Russian checkpoint, drenched and shivering.

~ * ~

"*Zurück!* Get back!" A stalking figure draped in a cape shouted at us through the thundering rain.

"*Guten Tag.*" *Mutti* tried to make contact taking a few steps toward the menacing shape.

"There's nothing good about this day," a voice as foul as the weather and whiskey heavy, answered in broken German. Now get back, *dumme Frau*, or I'll blow your head off."

Vati grabbed *Mutti's* arm and pulled her back into our midst, away from the threatening soldier.

Mutti pulled herself free of *Vati's* grasp and, holding her head high, she once more approached the Russian and bombarded him with words.

Still, he did not yield. He gave *Mutti* a shove, and *Mutti* turned to us and gave us the American wink. Flustered, she'd forgotten she was to tap

auf Wiedersehen

her nose to give us the sign to cry. Instead she flapped her wet eyelids up and down, frantically.

Petrified like two statues of stone we stood, Rosel and I, while *Vati*, Bienchen, and Hans looked on, waiting for us to cry. I did not have to think of sad things, for nothing could have been sadder than to see my proud mother reduced to a heap of jelly, begging and quivering, and still I could not cry.

Mutti, not to be denied her dream of a better life for us in the West, specifically in America, stopped batting her eyelids and, instead, she dropped to her knees in the mud and raised her steepled hands up to the angry sky, as if in prayer.

This so incensed the soldier he pulled the rifle off his shoulder and aimed it straight between her eyes. He pulled back the trigger, and grinned.

Our screams of terror swallowed by heart wrenching sobs, as predicted, reached a soft spot in the hardened Russian's soul. He stopped grinning, and gawked at us girls through bloodshot eyes. He let his arms drop then, releasing the trigger, and holding the rifle in one hand with its barrel down, he walked to the side of the road, and raised the barricade pole. "*Geh*." He yelled. Crazy Germans, go."

~ * ~

We ran, gasping for air, afraid the drunken Russian might have a change of heart and mow us down in no man's land, so close to our goal. We struggled in the knee-deep mud toward the American checkpoint, not far, and yet it seemed to take forever.

"Welcome to the West." The Americans greeted us and we collapsed into their open arms. They helped with our bags and led us to chairs, then brought us coffee and cakes, those funny little cakes with holes in the middle that tasted so good. "Have some more donuts," they said. I think Hans ate ten.

While we rested and collected the last grains of our strength, the sun pushed through the clouds of rain and sank into the fields, giving the land a golden misty glow.

18

Nestled between sloping forests of conifers, and spared from bombs, Osterode was very much like the towns of Germany that belonged to the world of Little Red Riding Hood, Snow-White, and all the other enchanting fairy-tale characters, created by the Brothers Grimm.

Red clay rooftops, sheltering buildings that dated back to the sixteenth century, crowded around the *Marktkirchturm*, the church-tower with its melodic resounding church-bells that beckoned the citizens of the town, each Sunday, to come and praise the Lord. Most of the people traveled through the cobblestone streets on foot, on bicycle, on scooter, or on a lightweight motorcycle, usually referred to as a bicycle with cough.

The air, pure with the scent of the surrounding evergreen forests, was tainted only once, each day, around five in the afternoon. Each day, when the church bells struck five, the chimney of the iron-works at the outskirts of town spit flames of fire like an angry dragon. The soot danced and drifted, like snowflakes, not white, but black, into every corner, outside and inside the building located within the iron-works yard, that would be our new home.

"So this is it?" *Mutti* dropped her bags. Her eyes roamed from the gray bumpy walls, to the cracked linoleum floor, to the wood burning cooking stove, to the table and four chairs. A cockroach flitted across the table.

"Where is the sink...? There is no sink...does that mean, there is no water in this place?" *Mutti* turned to *Vati*, and her eyes begged, please say it's not so.

In Apolda, although we had only one room, we did at least have water, down the hall. Except, of course, for the times when the water supply was in ill repair, which was quite often. In fact, we frequently had to pump water a few gardens away, and carry it home.

"But...we have electricity." *Vati* trying to mollify, turned on a switch to prove his claim.

"Hmm." Squinting at *Vati* through narrowed eyes, *Mutti* gave a tense nod of acknowledgment.

"We'll have to get the water from the shower house." Vati cleared his throat. "It's the first building...the building in the front, by the gates." *Vati* cleared his throat, again. "Or we can get it from the foundry, come see."

He cupped *Mutti's* elbow firmly, and led her to the door. "See? Right over there." He brought his face next to hers, and in a voice mixed with concern and persuasion, he continued. "That's the entrance to the big building with the chimney." He pointed to a place of darkness. "Right by the entrance is the water faucet. It's much closer than the shower stalls. Only a few steps, and," with his free hand he made a dramatic gesture. "Water galore."

Mutti backed away from *Vati*, stiff like a flagpole, and turned around. She walked, in slow motion as if under sedation, into the bedroom. Rosel and I followed.

auf Wiedersehen

"There're only two beds." I called out, and searched *Mutti's* face for an explanation. "They look awfully lumpy."

Mutti's face was empty, spent, all passion gone, and her eyes stared into space as she slumped against the wall.

Realizing it was best not to question her at this moment, I looked for a reaction from Bienchen. Bienchen and Hans hurried out of the bedroom, out of the kitchen door.

"We're going to the post office," Hans shouted over his shoulder, anxious to escape this dirt-hole, I could see.

"*Ja*," Bienchen added following Hans. "Maybe there is mail from our mother."

So I turned to *Vati*, whose eyes never left *Mutti's* vacant face, and I quickly said, hoping to break the looming silence between them, "those beds don't look so bad, after all…a little lumpy, maybe…but really, not so bad…as a matter of fact, they look pretty comfortable, if you ask me."

Rosel fell onto one of them and jumped back up, as if propelled by an explosive force, howling "o-u-c-h." She reached behind her, and got hold of something.

"That explains why they're so lumpy." Like a sword in her hand, she held out a piece of unyielding straw. "The mattresses are made of straw."

"Never mind the mattresses." *Mutti* found her voice again. Her eyes returned from space and met *Vati's* gaze. She pointed to a thin makeshift wall, on one side of the room. "What's behind there?" she demanded.

"Another room." Vati brought his finger over his lips.

Ignoring the sign of silence, she asked, "for us?"

Vati shook his head from side to side. "Nein…I'm afraid not. Four very nice Romanians live there…DP's…displaced persons who work here."

"Hmm." *Mutti* nodded as if she had not expected any other answer. Then pointing to the other side of the room, she asked, "and what's behind that wall?"

Vati hesitated. He cleared his throat, swallowed, cleared his throat, and finally said, "Lotte and Ludwig live there."

"Hmm." Again *Mutti* nodded, her face still void of any expression.

At last, she smiled with half her mouth and said, "I guess we are lucky then, to have two rooms when, the nice four young men only have one room, and Lotte and Ludwig only have one room too. Hmm."

She straightened then, a flicker of strength returned to her eyes, a quiver of smile returned to her lips, and she said, "We have to clean this place, before we settle in."

Vati heaved a sigh of relief and offered, "I'll get the water." Just as he reached the door, Mutti stopped him with one more question.

"Are Lotte and Ludwig also from Romania?"

"*Nein…*" Vati half turned around and, shrugged his shoulders in resignation. "Lotte and Ludwig are the horses that pull the finished iron products to the railway station, each week."

All *Mutti* said, was "Hmm."

19

Ah, life in the American Zone. Bienchen found a place with a family in need of a nanny. They had a spare room in their very fine home. Hans, who hoped to study architecture, took a job as an apprentice in a carpentry shop, where a room for him was available too.

Every day, except Saturday and Sunday, *Vati* had to deal, in temperatures over 110 °, with the molten iron glowing and flowing into fine molds. Rosel and I had to haul water, pail by pail, from the place of darkness, the entrance to the foundry. *Mutti* had her work to do with scrubbing, and scouring, and washing the curtains white as new.

A knock at the door interrupted her work, scrubbing the floor on all fours. "*Ja, wer ist denn da?*"

"*Guten* Morgen." *Fräulein* Gertrud, a robust bubbly young woman stood in the open doorway.

Mutti scrambled up from the floor, and put the pail and brush aside. She dried her red hands on the side of her *Kittelschürze*, apron dress, and invited *Fräulein* Gertrud to come in.

Fräulein Gertrud was one of *Herr* Burchard's maids. *Herr* Burchard, the owner of the iron works, kept several maids in his big house, which was located off to the side of the foundry's yard, facing a stream and footpath.

Fräulein Gertrud liked to drop in whenever she could get away. Besides a bag full of gossip, she always brought something to eat. Food was still very scarce, although we did have plenty of the American corn meal bread, which stuck to the sides of your throat like horse fodder.

The maid reached into the pouch of her gathered apron ends, and pulled out some rolls, a jar of marmalade, and a piece of smoked bacon. She placed them on the table and sat down on a wooden chair.

Mutti sat down opposite her and asked, "Are you sure *Herr* Burchard does not mind?" She would not accept, of course, stolen goods.

"Nein, *nein.*" She dismissed *Mutti's* worries with a wave of her hand, and mumbled under her breath. "That fat old *Arschloch* has more than enough."

"What did you say?" *Mutti* leaned forward in her chair.

"I said not to worry...about the food, I mean...It's from the provisions I get, which I never quite use up," *Fräulein* Gertrud cast her eyes down, and I could tell she was lying.

"You are too kind." *Mutti* reached across the table and grasped the young woman's hands. "I don't know how I will ever repay you."

A blush, like a shadow, ran over *Fräulein* Gertrud's cheeks. She sat back in her chair, pulled her hands free letting them glide over the smooth tablecloth, and changing the subject, she said, "I don't know how you do it...It's so...it's so *gemütlich* in here."

Mutti smiled, the type of smile that said you are most kind. *Fräulein* Gertrud leaned over the table then, and in a very low voice asked, "Did you hear that Herman is bringing his family?"

auf Wiedersehen

Mutti studied the young woman's face, feature-by-feature, and said, "You knew all along he was a married man, did you not?"

"*Ja*, but Herman told me he was getting divorced." She looked at *Mutti* with something very fragile in her eyes.

Mutti pinched her lower lip with her teeth, and she shook her head from side to side. "Men…hmm…"

She got up then and, with the dignity of a queen lost in a hopeless place, walked across the small kitchen, and placed the food in the old cabinet, the one *Vati had* found in the attic behind some straw. The straw, stored above our ceiling, was used to freshen up Lotte and Ludwig's beds. It was also the habitat of thousands of mice, of which several found their way each day through cracks into our rooms, adding to *Mutti's* everyday struggle to keep our home neat.

~ * ~

Lotte and Ludwig's soiled straw was heaped by Otto, the stable person, onto a dung mound, next to our building, and just in front of the out-house, the latrine, which we shared with the iron workers.

The latrine consisted of three compartments divided by wooden walls. The left side was where the men, shoulder-to-shoulder, let their waterspouts ring, while exchanging the latest rumors. The right side was where the men, haunch to haunch, did their thundering, while exchanging pleasantries. In the middle was our throne. It was hard to do what had to be done when battered, from both sides, with sounds of water torrents gushing, and thunder booming. You could, of course, hold your ears shut with your hands and soften the sounds. That is, if the peepholes were patched. If not, you needed your hands to cover them up.

However, I had devised a plan for privacy, which worked quite well for a time. Whenever I had to use the outhouse, just before entering, I would shout at the top of my lungs, "*Guten Tag, Herr* Burchard." The men would come streaming out of both sides. Their eyes roaming in search of their boss, and their fingers fumbling with their flies, they'd hurry into their workplace, the place of darkness, where the orange fire glowed and the iron flowed into molds, and into their spines.

20

"Why do we have to go to school?" I whined, dismayed by the prospect of being confined within four walls.

"Everyone has to go to school." Rosel gave an exasperated sigh. Obviously, she didn't mind.

"We didn't have to go in Apolda." I retorted, giving her a you-don't-know-everything look.

She deliberately exaggerated the disdain in her face, but before she could say anything more, *Mutti* intervened.

"Girls, girls, be quiet for a moment." She held a paper between her two hands and brought it up to her chest, as if to preserve the words in her heart.

Letting her eyes smile on my sister's face, she said. "I have here the doctor's report, Rosel. It says you will be fine. It says the TB was at a premature stage, and with proper care and nourishment you will continue to heal."

A sigh of relief escaped her lips. "It's a miracle. Here, where the air we breathe is filled with soot, and the water we drink is not pure, here…you heal?"

"It is…" Rosel's eyes clung to *Mutti's* face, analyzing her reaction. "It is a miracle."

"What do you mean?" *Mutti* narrowed her eyes in question.

"I mean…I…I asked God to make me well so you wouldn't have to worry any more." Rosel spoke the words with the certainty of someone who believes. "He is making me well."

Mutti wiped away a tear with the sleeve of her blouse, walked over to my sister, wrapped her into her arms, and whispered, "*Mein Kind.*"

I was overwhelmed. It was true. Rosel did not cough so much anymore. It was amazing. Maybe, if I asked God not to send me to school, I wouldn't have to go. Maybe it would work. Maybe…

Before I could further develop this thought, *Mutti* confronted me. "As for you, my child, of course you have to go to school. Consider yourself fortunate that, once again, you have the privilege of an education."

"But…but…"

"Tomorrow we'll meet your teacher, and no more buts about it."

~ * ~

Fräulein Hoffman, a spinster tall and haggard, with tiredness collected in the pockets under her eyes, ruled us with a stick. A stick she used to emphasize the words she squeaked onto the blackboard, a stick she used to emphasize obedience by whacking us across the back, or hands, or whatever part of body was accessible.

She taught us math, and reading, and writing, and science, and even gym and religion. Each week during our religion class the four Catholics, out of the forty students, were excused. They received instructions at another time, at another place from the local priest in his holy robe.

One day, at the start of religion class, when the sun and the whispering wind beckoned relentlessly outside the classroom window, I got up, as if in a trance, and attempted to leave with the Catholics.

auf Wiedersehen

"Are you *Catholisch* or *Evangelisch*?" *Fräulein* Hoffman's voice, a pitched stiletto, pushed me back into my seat. Her eyes pierced into my soul.

My soul wanted to hear only the song outside the window, and her question hung in the air, unanswered.

The crack of her stick coming down on her desk brought me back into the room.

"*Evantholisch*," I blurted out. I really didn't care what I was. I'd given up on God. *He was a big old meany*, I thought, *who didn't bother to answer a poor refugee kid's prayer.* I had prayed so hard. Please, dear God, don't make me go to school. Did he hear me? No. Why else would I have to be stuck in this stuffy room, full of stuffy Osterodean kids? Then again, Rosel was a poor refugee kid too. He listened to her. He was making her well. *Maybe I should give him another chance*, I thought. So I squeezed my eyes shut and prayed, as devout as I could. Please, dear God, let me be excused from religion class, so I can go outside and feel the sun and the wind on my face, which, by the way, you created for us in your infinite wisdom, and for which we thank you s-o-o-o much...

"So, *na ja*." *Fräulein* Hoffman said, tapping the stick in the palm of her hand and nearing my desk. "It seems we have a new religion. A religion founded by, no other than our new student, Christa Holder, who..." she slammed her stick on my desk, "is trying to get out of her religion class."

Laughter erupted in the classroom, and I slid down in my seat, hoping to disappear.

Just three seats up and to the right, Heiner turned around and looked at me.

I was acutely conscious of his mouth arched as if on the edge of laughter, and the way he held his head with cockiness. Indicating *Fräulein* Hoffman with his chin, he put his index finger to the side of his forehead and twisted it back and forth.

She turned around, unaware of the boy's insolence, and facing the four Catholics standing by the door, she dismissed them with a wave of her stick. "You may go." Turning back to me she said, "You stay."

Thus began the torture of memorizing endless Bible verses, without perceiving their virtue, and thus began a new friendship with Heiner.

"Hey," he said after class. Grabbing my books to carry them, he added, "I'll walk you home."

Heiner was not as tall as Lothar, another boy in my class who offered, a week before, to carry my books. Nor did he have chestnut curls. Lothar, the son of a forest ranger who lived in a chalet at the edge of the Harz mountains, was the handsomest boy my eyes ever got pleasure from until the day, that is, when he came to school, and his underpants showed below his Lederhosen. Besides, he too laughed when *Fräulein* Hoffman insulted me.

Heiner, on the other hand, had dared to be compassionate by giving the sign with the finger to his forehead, indicating *Fräulein* Hoffman is crazy. Had he been caught, he would have been disciplined, for sure, with whacks of the stick across the back.

Having flipped through my thoughts, I looked at Heiner then, with his thick crop of yellow hair, his blue eyes shone with merriment, and I smiled. I was in love again.

21

"*Um Gottes Willen, Junge*," *Mutti's* voice broke off in mid-sentence. "What happened to you?" She pulled my cousin Hans, followed by his sister, Bienchen, into the kitchen. It was Sunday, and as anticipated, Hans and Bienchen came for dinner.

I gaped at Hans, my mouth wide open, as bits and pieces of melodramatic scenes flashed across my mind. His handsome young face was reduced to half. The other half was a grotesque mask of pulp, through which squinted an eye, purplish black.

"It's nothing...don't worry..." he muttered, and allowed *Mutti* to lead him to the table, where she eased him into a chair.

Vati's eyes pored over him with high regard. "How did the other guy look?" he asked, his voice edged with awe.

"It wasn't like that." Hans looked slightly amused.

All ears were tuned in to him, but being the silent type who used words sparingly, Hans let his eyes do the talking most of the time, and now they were saying I'd rather not say.

"He got it in the ring. That's what happened," Bienchen burst out, throwing her hands up in disapproval. "He was knocked KO, tell them Hans."

"In the ring…? What do you mean…?" *Mutti* turned from Hans to Bienchen and back to Hans. "Hans, what's going on?"

"Hans took up boxing," Bienchen continued to answer for him. "To earn extra money, he lets himself be punched to a pulp." With a toss of her head, she whipped her shoulder length hair into place and the freckles scattered on her nose and cheeks, deepened in color.

"Is it true?" *Mutti* helped him peel off his jacket, ever so carefully in case he had more injuries. She handed it to Rosel. "Please put it away." Facing Hans, once more, she asked. "Is it true, Hans? You are boxing for money?"

"*Ja*…" Hans cleared his throat. "I need a suit…and new shoes…and… other things." He combed back his thick black hair with his fingers.

"Hans, you know nothing about boxing…you could get hurt...you are hurt." *Mutti's* eyes were wet with worry.

My heart thumped like a drum.

"Enough already…leave him alone…He'll be fine." *Vati* jabbed the air with his fists, first left, then right. Springing from foot to foot, he approached Hans, bobbing his head up and down, and side to side. "You just have to learn to duck, Hans…duck like so."

Hans just sat there, silent, knees wide taking up lots of room, leaving little space for *Vati's* pretend victory match.

The hush that followed was suddenly interrupted with loud neighing coming from behind the wall.

Vati exploded in laughter, and said, "Well at least Lotte agrees with me."

Hans, no longer able to keep a straight face, grimaced in pain as he too began to chuckle. As Lotte's neighs grew louder, so did our laughter.

With laughter casting the worries aside, at least for now, *Mutti* turned back to the stove where something was sizzling in the pan.

auf Wiedersehen

Sizzling, the sound that announced something scrumptious would be served, was an uncommon sound in our house.

Hans got up and peeked over *Mutti's* shoulder into the pan. He reached around her, and lifted the lid "M-mm...where did you get the ham from?" He inhaled deeply the rich luscious scent. "Burchard's maid? *Fraülein* Gertrud?"

"*Nein*..." *Mutti* shook her head.

Hans looked puzzled. "Not from the butcher...his shelves are empty." From the black market then? *Nein*..." Hans answered his own question. "It's illegal, and besides the prices are so inflated, no one can afford to go that route."

"That's for sure." *Mutti* smiled at him. "Most certainly not a poor refugee ironworker."

"Then how did you get the ham?" Hans scratched his head.

Mutti pushed her chin forward and pointed it toward *Vati*. "This poor iron worker, the actor, embezzled it."

Vati, forever optimistic and resourceful, started to visit the nearby farms on his days off, and entertained many a kindly farmer's plump wife with his theatrics.

They took great pity and, more than once, they were reduced to tears listening to his tales, which he sometimes replayed for us:

~ * ~

"*Ja ja*, times are hard...I have nine children, all crying out in the night from hunger."

"Ach, how terrible." The farmer's wife had dabbed at her eyes. "Here, take the milk and cottage cheese for the poor *Kinder*."

"*Ja ja*, times are hard...my mother, no longer right in the head, and bedridden, lives with us and is in dire need of nourishment."

"Ach, how terrible." The farmer's daughter patted his arm. "Here, take some bread and butter for poor little Grossmutter."

"*Ja ja*, times are hard…I have just lost my wife, raising two daughters by myself, and my heart longs for love."

"Ach, how terrible. Lord have pity on you." The farmer's mother-in-law held his face in both her hands and squeezed it between her voluminous breasts. "Here, take a cake and be sure to come back."

~ * ~

Who knows what melodramatic epic *Vati* pulled out of his bag of theatrics the day before. Whichever tale, it worked well, I could see as soon as he came in.

He waited until he had our full attention, and his infectious grin set the tone. This accomplished, he brought his hands to his chest, and flapped his elbows up and down, like a chicken flailing its wings.

"Cluck-cluck, cluck-cluck," he cackled like a hen and reached into the left pocket of his trouser pants, and laid an egg on the table.

"Cluck-cluck, cluck-cluck," he cackled again and reached into the right pocket of his trouser pants, and laid another egg on the table.

Mutti, cupped her face in her hands, and watched in astonished amusement as *Vati* cackled on.

Rosel and I joined in. "Cluck-cluck, cluck-cluck," we cackled like hens, and *Vati* brought forth more eggs, with shells not even cracked. Turning his pockets inside out empty at last, he stopped.

"One whole dozen?" *Mutti's* eyes widened with amazement.

Oh, I almost forgot." *Vati* reached, one more time, into an overlooked pocket and pulled out a slab of ham.

auf Wiedersehen

~ * ~

I let my tongue slide around my lips in anticipation of savoring the ham, still sizzling in the pan. I tried to remember if I had ever tasted ham before, but I could not. Without being asked, I set the table. *Vati* brought in crates to serve as extra chairs. Rosel placed the silverware. Bienchen lit the candles. At last, *Mutti* was finished cooking and started to serve the potatoes, cabbage, ham and eggs.

Our spirits were high as we crowded around the small kitchen table to start the feast. Just as my fork, pitching a mouth-watering piece of ham, was half way to my lips, there was a tap at the door.

"*Ja? Wer ist denn da?*" *Mutti* got up, opened the door, and gasped. "Duh?"

22

The stranger hesitated in the open doorway. She straightened her shoulders and cleared her throat, but no words came from her lips. The glow on her cheeks was like the glow of sunset on snow. Her hair, windblown, and black like a starless night, was like the hair of a bedraggled Snow-White. Opening her arms, she managed to whisper through stiff lips, "Hans…Bienchen…"

Bienchen jumped up, and flung her arms around her mother's neck. Hans just sat there and stared. I quickly shoved the piece of ham between my teeth, realizing in all the commotion that followed, there was one more mouth to feed.

Hans and Bienchen's mother, the Snow-White look-alike, the one that had been spoiled by their mother, our *Oma* Machein, the scientific miracle who had lived without a stomach for quite a while before she died, *Tante* Lieschen had arrived.

Mutti, with tears blinding her eyes and choking her voice, pulled her older sister into the kitchen, mumbling again and again, "Lieschen…Lieschen…"

auf Wiedersehen

~ * ~

Together with *Mutti*, *Tante* Lieschen found a two-room attic apartment, up the hill, not too far. While fall faded into winter, and winter into spring, we often went visiting.

"I like going to *Tante* Lieschen's place," I said, catching my breath, trying to keep in step with *Mutti's* long legs, as we walked up the hill one day.

"I know…" She patted my head. "She plays make-up with you…and you like that."

"*Ja.*" I smiled, thinking of all the remarkable things I found in Tante Lieschen's bedroom dresser, lipstick, eyebrow liner, mascara, powder, rouge, and toilet water, treasures *Mutti* did not possess.

Bienchen and Hans were sitting by the table, when we arrived, poring through a family album. *Mutti*, *Vati*, and Rosel joined them, but I headed for the bedroom where *Tante* Lieschen sat on the bed, brushing her hair.

"If I brush your hair," I climbed on the bed and knelt behind her, "can I make up your face again?" I took the brush from her and let it glide down her raven hair.

"M-m-m…" she nodded with a sigh. "First brush some more."

Soon my arms grew tired. I piled her hair up on top of her head, and twisted it into a bird's nest. "*Schick*," I proclaimed.

"*Schick*, indeed," *Tante* Lieschen agreed, turning her head from left to right in front of the mirror. "I look like Cleopatra."

"Who's Cleopatra?" I wanted to know.

"She was an Egyptian Queen who reigned long ago." *Tante* Lieschen picked up the brush. "Come on, it's your turn to be made into a queen." She undid my braids, brushed out the waves, and combed one side behind the ear, and one side half over the eye. She stepped back then and let her eyes slide over me. "H-m-m...it's not so much the Cleopatra-look, it's more the Marlene Dietrich-look."

I walked to the mirror and looked at myself. I was pleased.

"*Schön*, don't you think?" *Tante* Lieschen stepped behind me and looked at my reflection in the mirror. "You have more than looks in common... did you know Marlene Dietrich went to America and became an American?"

"Really?" I was intrigued. "I think we are going, too. *Mutti* received another letter from her friend. A big package came a few days ago."

"*Ja,* I know." *Tante* Lieschen stepped back and paused for a moment thoughtfully. "Anyway, when Hitler wanted Marlene Dietrich to come back to Germany she refused."

"Wow...I bet he didn't like that."

"Not at all...to anger him even more, she entertained the American troops, and gave anti-Nazi broadcasts in German."

"Really...? Can we do the make-up now?"

We applied lots and lots of make-up on each other, and when we were finished, we exited from the bedroom and presented ourselves to the rest of the family. "Ta-rah."

"A-a-h" and "O-o-h..." they raved and looked amused, all except *Mutti*.

"You look like ladies from the *Reeperbahn*." She shook her head, and pulled up one side of her mouth, more in scorn than in a smile. "Will you please go and wash it off?"

Although I did not know at the time that the *Reeperbahn* was the mile of sin in Hamburg, and the ladies my mother referred to were paid whores, I could tell by the tone of her voice, she did not approve. Nevertheless *Tante* Lieschen and I, having worked on each other with

auf Wiedersehen

such diligence and care, knew we looked divine, and ignored *Mutti's* request for as long as we could, all through supper.

All through supper, the silence and tension grew thick like a fog no one could penetrate, except *Vati*. He leaned across the table and looked at *Tante* Lieschen and said, "Would you please be so kind and pass the bread, Daughter of the last Pharaoh, Cleopatra Divine?"

23

"Look." *Tante* Lieschen pointed to a family portrait in the album she brought along. It had been their turn to visit us, and we were seated around the kitchen table. "Look…how August smiles at Augustine."

"Who are August and Augustine?" I asked, feeling a grin coming up. The names reminded me of the Vienna folk song, *Ach Du lieber Augustin, Augustin, Augustin…*

"August and Augustine were our parents," *Tante* Lieschen explained in a voice that trailed to a place far away. "They were so in love…really…more so than most married couples."

"What happened to *Tante* Lotte?" Hans pointed to a young woman in another snapshot. "She was the oldest sister, was she not?" *Lotte had legs as sturdy as Lotte's next door,* I thought, glancing at the young woman in the photograph. Of course, she had only two legs, instead of four.

"The last I heard she was still in Königsberg." *Tante* Lieschen said her voice edged with concern.

Mutti, who sat next to *Tante* Lieschen, stroked the photograph with her fingertips before turning the page. "I hope Lotte will be all right…you say she has to cook for them…for the Russians?"

auf Wiedersehen

"*Ja*...One time, Lotte told me, she set a very nice table for them," *Tante* Lieschen went on. "She brought out a linen tablecloth, good china, and fine silverware. The Russians were grateful and in awe, but never touched the silverware. Instead, they pushed it aside and used their fingers like barbarians."

"Tsk...Tsk..." *Mutti* tsked. "They must have been from the countryside. People from Moscow, I'm sure, are civilized..."

Rosel, who listened attentively, leaned forward and turned the page back. She pointed to August and Augustine and asked, "You mean *Oma* Machein is Augustine...? The one without the stomach...?" Her eyebrows rose in obvious puzzlement.

"*Ja ja*...one and the same...look how well dressed she is...she always paid such attention to her appearance..." *Mutti* put her arm around her sister's shoulder. "You, *Lieschen*, are a lot like her, I think."

"*Ja*..." Tante Lieschen smiled. "You are more like August, I think. Remember how he always paid more attention to the feet. 'The feet are more important than the face,' he'd say and bathe and massage Augustine's feet."

"Was August a scientific miracle too?" I asked. "A medical breakthrough?"

"*Nein*..." *Mutti* sighed. "August fell off a wagon while pitching hay, and cracked his skull wide open. There was nothing science could do for him."

"Enough of this." Tante Lieschen closed the album with a bang. "Let's play Romme."

It was during the Romme game I realized *Mutti*, whose principles competed with the principles of Pope Pius, lost all sense of morality when it came to cards.

"You cheated," *Tante* Lieschen exclaimed, her voice furious, after *Mutti* won another round.

"I did not," *Mutti* insisted, her sapphire eyes brimming with innocence, while collecting the pennies.

"*Aber Tante* Anna...really..." Hans looked at *Mutti*, creasing his brows in disapproval.

Mutti directed her innocent eyes at him and asserted, "I did not...really...you must believe me."

"*Tante* Anna, you did so." Bienchen grinned, bringing her dimples to life. "Shame on you."

"*Nein*, I did not," *Mutti* persisted, as casually as she could manage. Shuffling the cards and dealing out another hand, she looked at *Tante* Lieschen with eyes turning from innocence to amusement, and asked, "Are you in or out?"

In the corner *Vati*, who never played cards with us, chuckled and continued to sprinkle tobacco into a small thin piece of paper. He rolled the tobacco inside the paper between his calloused fingers, delicately, back and forth, and back and forth. When satisfied with its roundness and size, he let his tongue slide along the edge of the paper then tapped it down with his fingertips to make it stick. Holding the freshly rolled cigarette at arm's length, he admired it like a prize then stuck it between his lips and lit a match to it. Through the smoke he watched us and smiled.

I pulled my eyes from *Vati's* pre-occupation with his cigarette, and let them rest on my mother's face. Could it be, I wondered? Could it be my mother, who I adored and held in such high esteem, was a cheat, a liar, and a card shark? I stared at her with deadly concentration, and *Mutti's* eyes squinted in guilty embarrassment.

"You did so," I blurted out with righteous anger, and slammed my palms down on the table.

No longer able to sustain the pretense of innocence, *Mutti* lost her composure and started to giggle.

"*Mutti*, you didn't, did you?" Rosel, still hoping our mother was not a cheat, received as answer a sheepish smile.

Hans threw his hand of cards into the air, and grunted, "Devil's game."

Thus, another card game ended, and *Mutti* escaped her lie by bringing out the bread and the can of Crisco, the funny tasting bread spread that came in the friend's package from America.

That night, after Rosel and I crept into our straw beds, we listened to the adults talk as once again they flipped through the album of memories.

24

"Look Lieschen, here's Gerda and her husband Erwin...Look, how handsome Erwin is in his flyer's uniform...and how proud Gerda looks up to him."

"Yes, but that was a while ago. Erwin got shot down and his face is all messed up. I think they are getting divorced."

"Why?" *Mutti* asked. "Because he no longer is handsome?"

"What about their children, Bärbel and Jörg?

"Who knows...war does strange things to people...I think the children are in a children's home."

"Tsk...tsk...Mutti tsked. That child of our sister was always spoiled."

"Isn't this Horst, our cousin?" They must have flipped to another page. "Oh what a charmer he was. Do you remember, Lieschen?"

"Do I ever, all the girls in Königsberg were in love with him."

"Yes, I remember...I never could figure out why or how...He was not the tallest or handsomest young man around...but he did have such charisma..."

"I know...he so charmed all the ladies."

"So where is he now?"

"You haven't heard?"

"Heard what?"

"The last time he came home on furlough, his mother could tell from the start something was wrong with her son.

"What do you mean?"

"He didn't call any of his lady friends…he didn't laugh…he didn't eat…he had become a morose young man."

"Horst…remorse…? Impossible."

"It's true…when his mother tried to find out what happened to him, at first he refused to talk. Eventually though, before he was to return to duty, he let things slip out."

"What do you mean?" *Mutti* asked. "What slipped out?"

"All I know he had been assigned to serve at a place called Treblinka."

"There are terrible rumors going around about Treblinka." I heard my mother suck in air. "Supposedly, Treblinka is an extermination camp where, with the help of the Ukrainians, thousands of Jews were murdered."

"I am afraid, dear sister, they are not just rumors …according to what Horst told his mother just before…"

"Just before what?"

"Just before he was to return to duty, they went on an outing to the Baltic Sea."

"They must have gone to the place we always came together, remember, before the war?

"Yes, I think that's where they went hoping to recapture some of the old happiness. On the last day of the holiday, Horst walked into the sea and never returned…"

25

"Look, the swallows," I shouted, approaching the stable next door. "Look how they swoop, so low, back and forth, like scissors flashing they slice the air."

"*J-a-a*...the swallows are back." Otto, the stable person, tall, rawboned, with a broad appealing face, pulled out a hanky from his back trouser pocket and wiped his forehead before readjusting his cap on his ruffled hair. He pitched more fresh straw into Ludwig and Lotte's beds. And Lotte turned her head on her long thick neck and watched and neighed, as if to say thanks.

"Come look," I said, standing in the open door. "Come look, and watch the swallow waltz."

Otto stopped pitching straw and stepped out of the stall. He pointed to a spot below the roof. "See? They built a nest for their young ones under the overhang."

"A fine place they picked," I said. "If I were one of their young ones, I'd rather be raised in America ...you know...the country of milk and honey."

"*J-a-a*...well...swallows don't like milk or honey...they like bugs...and we got plenty of them around here...thanks to Lotte and

auf Wiedersehen

Ludwig." Otto walked back into Lotte's stall and resumed pitching straw. "That's why they return each year."

"Where do they come from…and where do they go each year…the swallows, I mean?"

"They take flight to the warmer south." Otto lowered his voice to make it sound suspenseful. "They fly ten thousand kilometers down to Africa. There they fly over mountains like the Pyrenees, which are more than three thousand meters high."

"Really?" I was amazed.

"Really, I read about it once." Otto pushed back his cap and scratched his head before going on. "They fly over the Sahara where they scarcely find any water. After weeks they reach their destination for their winter accommodation. In the spring they leave again, and wing their way back here."

"I'm glad they come back each year," I said pulling my eyes away from them. I walked into Lotte's stall then and let my hand glide along her wide pallid flank.

"Why does Lotte look so sad?" I asked. "Why are her ears, one forward and one back, like that?"

"Ach…she's not sad." Otto stopped freshening up her bed, and leaning on the pitchfork, he thought for a minute before he said, "She just acts like an old mare, which she is, of course…and she can't see you coming up from the rear."

"What do you mean?"

"She has a blind spot directly behind and directly in front. When her ears are like that it means she's in doubt."

"Really?" The tenderness in his voice did not surprise me. It was obvious Otto loved his horses.

"Talk to her…let her know you are her friend," he advised.

"I like you, Lotte," I said. "You are the most beautiful mare in the whole wide world." I walked to the front of the stall, and she picked up her head.

"When her head is up like that, she can see you when you are near. When her head is down, she can see you far."

"I didn't know that. You know a lot about horses," I said. "About swallows, too," I added as an afterthought.

"*J-a-a...see?*" Otto pointed to her ears. "See how her ears are pricked forward now? She's happy...she likes you."

I looked at Lotte's ears, and sure enough they both were pointed forward.

"When the ears are flattened back against her head, she's unhappy," Otto explained. "If one ear is pricked forward, and one ear held back, she's in doubt. If both ears are pricked forward, like now, she's happy."

"Her eyes still look sad," I pointed out. "I think she doesn't like to be cooped up in here all the time."

"*J-a-a...*well...that's just the way it is. Lotte and Ludwig are workhorses. They're no worse off than those poor Trottel in there." Otto stopped spreading the straw and pointed out the door to the building with its tall chimney.

I walked to where Otto stood, and followed his gaze to the smokestack spewing sparks of fire and ashes.

"Those poor suckers are breaking their backs for a few lousy Marks while Burchard's wallet and his *Arsch* get fatter all the time." Otto's tongue was heavy with sarcasm. He aimed a glob of spit in a high curve out the door.

I was impressed. I tried to do the same, but missed and hit poor Lotte's hind flank. Lotte craned her head back and looked at me with those big, deep, brown colored eyes. So I quickly wiped it clean with the palm of my hand. Lotte moved her head up and down and neighed.

auf Wiedersehen

I turned my attention back to Otto then. "What do you mean...those poor Trottel?"

"*Ach*... never mind. This weekend they'll celebrate. Saturday is May Day, you know. You can ride with me on the wagon in the parade."

"Really...? I can't wait...where will the parade go?"

"Along the main street to the *Marktplatz*, where the festivities will take place. You know...dancing, singing, and speeches too, under the May Pole."

"Why do they always have a May Pole with streamers and all?"

"The pole is the skyward symbol of life. The streamers add color. They're held by the men and women while they dance around the pole."

"I can't wait. I never celebrated May Day before."

"You'll like it, I'm sure." Otto patted my head in passing to the other side of the stall. "It's a day of gladness for the workers, a celebration of the coming of summer."

"Are you sure I can ride with you?"

"*Ja*...I already asked Burchard, and he said you could. You just have to ask your mother. You can help me get Lotte and Ludwig spruced up."

"I will...we'll make them look magnificent. We'll brush their coats until they shine like...like the stars at night. We can put wreaths of flowers around Lotte and Ludwig's necks. And we can..."

"*Ja, ja-a-a*...we'll do all that. When we are finished with them, they'll look like show horses and they'll forget they are draft horses...at least for the day." Otto took a brush from the covered bench and combed Lotte's thick mane, and her tail went up.

"Look at her tail." Otto pointed the brush toward Lotte's hindmost. "Look how she holds her tail high. That too means she's in a good mood." Lotte did a resounding fluff and messed up her freshly made up bed.

Otto shook his head from side to side. "It can also mean that." He laughed, and Lotte whinnied, which made Otto laugh even harder.

26

"*Mutti*, can I ride with Otto in the May Day Parade?" I asked as I burst into the kitchen. "He says I can, if you say it's all right…Can I…Can I, please?"

"*Um Gottes Willen, Kind*. You smell like a horse." Mutti moved back and fanned the air with her hand in front of her nose.

"Can I, Mutti, please?" I persisted stepping close to her face batting my eyelashes at a frantic pace.

"We'll talk about it after you take a shower." She handed me a towel and a bar of castile soap. "The men will be finished by now." She looked at the clock on the wall. "*Ja*, they'll all have gone home by now. Quick…Go take a shower."

I ran across the iron-works yard, anticipation rising to explosion force. I knew I could convince *Mutti* to let me be in the parade.

I entered the shower room. The air was dense from fungus growth. A row of stained steel sinks lined the wall on one side of the room. On the other side were two shower stalls. The door to the stall on the left was closed.

"Hallo?" I said. "Is anyone here?" No one answered. No one was here.

auf Wiedersehen

I clomped my wooden clogs on the concrete floor. I had overheard the maid, *Fraulein* Gertrud say, that one of the men had been attacked by a rat while taking a shower not long ago. Clomp...clomp ...clomp...I scared the rats away.

Just as I was about to enter the shower stall on the right, the door of the left stall opened somewhat. In the dark shadows stood a man with a towel draped around his hips. He gave it a yank and let it fall.

I stood, stunned, frozen, paralyzed.

The man's private part was quite large. I had seen only one other before, the day I had played with Günter in the yard, and he had aimed his little waterspout at the freshly painted wooden gate.

Run...an inner voice whispered, but my feet were glued to the floor. Run...my inner voice persisted, and still I could not move. I glanced up into the man's face, a stranger's face.

Drops of moisture clung to his forehead, and his eyes, glassy and veiled, stared into nothingness.

He made no threatening move toward me, but his hand took hold of his you-know-what and he started to pump it, slowly at first. Escalating his endeavor in speed and force, it became even larger, I thought.

Run...run...run...the thunderous roar of my inner voice reverberated in my head.

Still I could not move.

The man reached a savage speed when at last he shuddered and gave it a final jerk. Without so much as saying a word, he picked up his towel and wrapped himself, then hurried out the door.

I at last stepped through the wall of ice that kept me paralyzed, and into the other stall. I slammed the door shut. I jammed the bolt locked. I turned the showerhead on. I tore my clothes off. I let the water wash away the sensation of confusion and shame. After a very long time, I rubbed my skin dry, got dressed, and stood very still. The only sound was the drip, drip, drip, echoing off the concrete walls.

I opened the door a tiny bit, and made my eyes investigate. The man had not returned. Letting out a sigh of relief, I clomped to a sink to brush my teeth. A cockroach disappeared down the drain. I turned the hot water on, full force, and gritted my teeth. "Breathe your last breath *Kakerlak*," I rasped.

27

"You are so quiet, Christa. It's not like you." *Mutti* put her pen down and picked up her glasses, which as usual lay idle next to her writing pad. She turned around and looked at me. "Is anything wrong?"

I thought of telling her about the stranger in the shower, how it made me feel confused and scared. Maybe she would shush me, the way she always had, and say, "Don't worry, child…everything will be fine." Then Rosel came in and instead I asked, "Who you writing to?"

"Paul Westendorf, our friend in America. He wants you girls to come and live with his sister and her husband." She reached out and seized my hand. "They live on a big farm in a small town in upstate New York, and they have no children." *Mutti* pulled me onto her lap and stroked my back.

"What did you tell him?" Rosel asked as she approached, lips puckered with suspicion.

"I told him no. I told him we would never part, either we all come, or no one at all."

"What do you think he'll say?" I twisted around on *Mutti's* lap and studied her face. I tried to imagine what it might be like to live somewhere without her, to live somewhere with strangers. "Do they have horses?" I wondered out loud.

"I know they have cows…lots of them…but I don't know if they have horses." *Mutti's* eyes narrowed in question. "Why do you ask?"

"I don't know…horses are better than cows…like Lotte and Ludwig, they're clever. Especially Lotte."

"What does it matter?" Rosel asked mockingly. "We're not going…I'm not going to live on some stupid farm with strangers." A look of despair spread over her face.

"No one said you would, Rosel." *Mutti* spoke calmly and her eyes smiled at her oldest child.

Rosel stood there, pacified, at least for now. Her long thick braids gleamed golden on top of the cornflower blue blouse that strained against her young developing chest. No longer fragile and sickly, one could detect a hint of the woman Rosel was becoming, wholesome and lovely.

"Hmm…speaking of horses…" *Mutti's* forefinger traced the ridge of my nose. "I talked to *Vati*…you can ride in the May Day Parade. You too, Rosel, if you like."

Rosel declined, "No thanks, I don't share Christa's interest in horses." Picking up a book, she walked into the bedroom.

Not having anything better to do, I got up and followed her. She was not reading. Her book lay open on her chest. Her legs were crossed, her interlaced fingers were tucked beneath her head, and her eyes strained at the ceiling.

"Is something wrong?" I asked.

"*Nein*, leave me alone." Her eyes sought mine for a moment, and I thought I detected something like confusion and shame.

"Why won't you tell me?" There was a creeping uneasiness at the bottom of my heart. "I can see something is wrong," I persisted.

She turned away from me and remained silent.

"I think sisters should tell each other everything, don't you agree? Maybe I want to tell you something too, maybe…"

auf Wiedersehen

She turned around then and looked at me with those grave blue eyes, as if the thought of telling me tore at her insides. "Some things are too hard to tell." She sighed. She did not tell me, at least not then…

~ * ~

Blissfully wrapped in God's holy grace, Rosel was coming home from her confirmation class. She walked through the gates into the iron-works yard when from the opposite direction one of the DP's, one of the young Romanians, approached. She smiled and said "*Guten Tag*."

He smiled back, making his eyes rove over her.

A flash of warning and fear gripped her, but it was too late. He lunged for her, pulled her into the horses' quarters, and pushed her against the wall. She resisted and struggled and tried to break free, but she was no match for the aroused young man. He just laughed, seized her hands, and pinned them behind her back. No longer able to fight, she begged, "please don't…please, let me go." He silenced her by pressing his lips on hers, and forcing his tongue inside her mouth. Keeping her pinned with one hand against the wall, and muttering soothing words, he unbuttoned his fly and hiked up her skirt when, suddenly, out of nowhere Otto appeared waving his pitchfork.

"I'll kill you, so help me God," Otto yelled, " If I ever see you near one of the girls again, I'll kill you, I swear."

The young Romanian gasped. "I was not going to hurt her," he stammered. Fear, severe and vivid, glittered in his eyes as he fled.

With Otto as our guardian angel, our protector, our friend, my sister and I were never disgraced again while living in the iron-works yard. After a while we relaxed, and no longer looked with trepidation at every man. After a while, life became beautiful again.

28

"*Ja*, come in." *Mutti* dried her hands on the ends of her apron. She opened the door, and *Fräulein* Gertrud walked in with her arms precariously filled with goods. Having placed them on the table, she pulled out a picture from the pocket of her blouse and held it out to me. "*Schau*…a picture of you in the May Day parade with Otto and Lotte and Ludwig."

"*Toll*." I looked at the picture with admiration. "Lotte and Ludwig look so…so stately all decked out in their festive gear. Who took the photograph?" I asked.

"Heinz…you know…the big guy." Her words rang with happiness. Turning to *Mutti* she said, in a lowered voice, "I took your advice…I stopped seeing Herman a while ago…and I went to the May Day parade with Heinz."

"I'm glad." *Mutti* gave her a smile, a motherly kind of smile. "Someone always ends up hurt in triangles like that, you know. Besides, Heinz is much more intelligent, much nicer all around."

I wondered what she meant by triangles like that…something to do with Herman, the married guy, I guessed. Heinz was a nice guy all right, single, intelligent, but also a clumsy *Klotz*.

"*Ja,* he is very intelligent," *Fräulein* Gertrud agreed, pride gleaming in her eyes. "He went to the University, you know." She nodded her head to confirm it was so. "Did you know he applied to immigrate to Canada? Maybe, he'll ask me to go with him."

"Would you go, if he asked?" *Mutti* started to store the goods in the cabinet.

"*Ja,* I think I would. No more washing, no more scrubbing, no more bowing to Burchard's demands. Ja, I would go."

"Hmm…in Canada you could start a new life, just as we could in America." *Mutti* patted *Fräulein* Gertrud's frizzy permed head.

"That reminds me…" The maid pulled a letter from her apron pocket. "I almost forgot. This is for you."

Mutti looked at the familiar envelope edged in red and blue with its multiple airmail stamps on top. "It's from our friend, Paul Westendorf." She inhaled a long deep breath, tore open the envelope, and let her eyes skim down the lines. Sunshine broke across her face half way down the page. "He says we can come." Her voice broke off. After skimming down further, she went on in a whisper. "He says he'll sponsor us. Imagine that. All of us." A sob escaped her trembling lips, as she collapsed into herself.

I listened in silence, happy yet sad, since once again, in time to come, I'd have to say *auf Wiedersehen* to my friends. I remembered then, I was to meet my friend Heiner at the swimming pool.

"Can I go swimming, *Mutti*?" I asked.

"*Ja ja*, run along…but be careful…don't go in the deep end…" *Mutti's* concerned voice trailed after me.

~ * ~

The sky glared hot and blue. School was closed for the summer, and we kids spent our days in the town's outdoor pool.

Heiner looked devilishly handsome in his tiny bathing suit. "Let's go for a swim." He reached for me, his arms silky with hairs, and pulled me up from the blanket we shared. Hand-in-hand, we walked to the edge of the pool. Although not very tall, Heiner was sinewy and strong for someone so young. Almost eleven, he was a few months older than I. His blond hair, streaked white by the summer sun, deepened his tan. I could see the girls, my friends, giving him the eye, especially Heidi, who I think was his girl before me.

~ * ~

I liked Heidi a lot. She was the joker in our classroom, always pulling stunts and making us laugh. Besides, she knew more about sex and such things, and willingly shared her knowledge with the rest of us, who still puzzled over this mystery. She was the one who had noticed an older classmate had grown quite fat before disappearing for a few months. When she returned, the classmate that is, Heidi noticed she was not so fat anymore. "You know what that means," Heidi said, her voice edged with wisdom.

"She went on a diet?" I asked, wondering where and how one would have access to so much food as to grow fat. I was still hungry a lot. Her father perhaps, or grandfather I supposed, must be a farmer.

"*Nein*, she didn't diet." Heidi grinned and used her hands to show an imaginary huge stomach. She tried to clarify, "a baby, silly...she did you- know-what with a guy."

auf Wiedersehen

Although I no longer believed the stork delivered babies, I had no clue as to what our classmate did with a guy. I considered telling Heidi about the man in the shower, letting her know I was not entirely ignorant of such things. So far it had not felt right, to tell her about it, I mean. Besides, Heidi's stories, whether real or imaginary, were always funny. My story was not funny at all. Maybe she would tell her mother, and maybe her mother would tell my mother, and maybe…

"Want to go and jump off the high diving board?" Heiner's voice broke into my thoughts.

"I don't know…" I hesitated. "I never tried before." I let my eyes skim across the pool, over the bobbing heads of people frolicking in the water, to the high diving board on the other side.

"Come on…" Heiner squeezed my hand and his eyes, full of merriment, encouraged me. He pulled me toward the other side of the pool. "It's not so hard…I'll show you how."

I stood at the bottom of the diving board and looked up. "It's awfully high…I don't know…maybe I better not."

Heiner, with his hand on my back, firmly coaxed me up, and up, and up. "Don't worry…I'm right behind you." His voice reached my ears but not my mind.

At last on top, I dared to look down and realized with shock it seemed even higher from up here than from down there. I held on to the side bars and, cautiously, took a step forward, and another, and another, until I reached the end of the board. Heiner, still right behind me, beamed and waved to the group of girls gathered below.

"*Gut*," he said, turning his attention back to me. "Now all you have to do is reach for your toes and push off with your feet."

I squinted my eyes at the distant deep. Panic was rioting within me. Half turning around, I hoped for retreat.

"Put you arms straight up, one on each side of your head and interlock your thumbs." Heiner waited, challenging me to follow his instructions.

I swallowed hard, lifted my arms, and forbade myself to tremble.

"*Gut.*" He placed one hand on my upper back easing me forward and down. The other hand he placed on top of my feet holding them into place. While my heart thumped against my rib cage, he gave me a shove and…I soared, and I soared, and I soared like a bird, engulfed in a breeze of freedom and bliss, and with a swish, I disappeared into the dark refreshing deep. Surfacing, I looked up at my hero and watched as he bounced up and down on the board, then in a high wide arc dove in after me.

I held my breath waiting for him to come up, eager to tell him how fantastic it was, but he surfaced at the edge of the pool and smiled at the group of girls who watched. Just as I was about to be overcome by waves of jealousy, he pushed off the edge of the pool and swam back to me with long graceful strokes.

"Hmm," I said.

"Hmm," he said. "Let's go and get a lemonade."

29

"*Würstchen*…we're having *Würstchen* for dinner?" I inhaled the scrumptious scent that rose in a vaporous cloud over the sizzling sausages in the pan. "Mm…where did we get them from?" I asked, directing my eyes at *Mutti*.

Mutti pretended not to hear and wiped away tears with the sleeve of her blouse. Picking up the knife, once more, she continued to peel the onion.

Hans, who had overheard my question as he walked in, grinned and said, "They came from the horse, the horse that was…"

"Hans," *Mutti* stopped him short, sending a reproachful look my cousin's way. Then turning to me and to Rosel, she explained, "It's horsemeat…it's perfectly fine to eat horsemeat." When she saw the crease between Rosel's eyes deepening, she added. "It's protein, you know. Protein's essential for growing bones, and your bones are still growing. Besides, in some countries, horsemeat is considered a delicacy."

That was good enough for me. Attacked by hunger pangs, reinforced by the aroma, I couldn't wait to taste this fine delicacy. Rosel, who was setting the table, remained skeptical, I could tell by her face.

"*Ja-a-a...*" Hans nodded in agreement. The look on his face changed to all seriousness. "Your mother is right...it's a real treat...and afterwards," a note of mockery now crept into his voice, "we'll neigh like so, *hü-ü-ü-ü-ü.*"

"Enough already, Hans." *Mutti* flashed him an angry look, then walked to the stove and turned the sausages in the pan. "How are your studies coming along?" she asked over her shoulder, changing the subject.

Behind her back, Hans sent me a conspiratorial message with his eyes, saying, it's really so...just wait and see. To *Mutti* he said, "*Gut*, I'm glad I chose the field of architecture. I think I'll like being an architect."

"*Ja*, designing houses will be a nice profession." *Mutti* turned around and, seeing his wide shoulders strain against his white shirt, she smiled and added. "You'll be able to design and build them too. Maybe, some day, you'll build a house for us in America...a house with a toilet inside...with a shower and a bathtub, too...*ach,* to soak in a *Schaumbad* again...what luxury that will be."

"With lots of windows," I chimed in. "Lots of windows to let the sun shine in...and with shutters that rattle when the wind is angry."

"We don't need our own house." Rosel looked at *Mutti*. "We'll live in the mansion with your friend, the mansion by the river, remember?"

"*Ja ja*," *Mutti* agreed with my sister and then turned to Hans. "Are your mother and sister coming?" she asked.

"*Nein...*" He hesitated for a moment, as if considering whether or not to say what he wanted to say, then spluttered through suppressed laughter. "*Nein*...they're afraid they might start to...you know...*hü-ü-ü-ü-ü.*"

Rosel flashed him a condescending look that said, *Ja*, sure, in your dreams. This prompted Hans, with his back to *Mutti* and his hands cupped over his mouth, to one more time go "*hü-ü-ü-ü-ü.*"

auf Wiedersehen

"*Hör auf,* Hans." Mutti breathed an exasperated sigh. "Enough already… no more…enough with the nonsense."

"S-h-h-h-h-h." *Vati* was fiddling with the knob on the little radio that whined and beeped and made all kinds of sounds except music. He acquired it for five Mark from a co-iron worker.

Mutti had been furious. "We cannot afford such luxuries," she scolded. "You know we must save every penny for our trip to America."

"*Ach*," *Vati* answered. "We have plenty of time to save. With the idiotic bureaucracy involved, it'll take forever to get our immigration papers. In the meantime, we can listen to the news…we can listen to Mozart…we can listen to…*Scheiss* Radio." *Vati* exploded and whacked the small black box with the palm of his hand. "No wonder he wanted so little for it. It's a piece of junk." He gesticulated into space.

"Here…let me try…" Hans offered. Placing his hand on *Vati's* shoulder and nudging him gently aside, he played with the knob. One turn forward, two turns back, one half turn forward, and the room flooded with the melodic tune of the Blue Danube Waltz.

Hans was master at everything, I thought. *Well, maybe not at boxing.* I recalled his black puffy eye, *but at everything else.* Of course he was teasing, I reasoned, about the neighing, I mean. Then again, he was not the teasing kind. He was more the silent, serious type, like *Mutti,* in many ways. They shared, of course, the same Prussian ancestors, the same *Oma* Machein, the one who lived without a stomach for quite a while. Thinking of stomachs, it came to mind the last time we ate the ham *Vati* embezzled from the kindly farmer's wife, we all developed tapeworms. When the bitter horseradish we were forced to eat in huge quantities did not rid us of those slimy things that grew into endless lengths, we had to go to the doctor who gave us pills and said, "Examine your stools meticulously, and make sure you see the head when it comes out…If the head remains, it'll grow back to full size again." What an ordeal that had been, pooping into a pail for days, hoping to come face to face with that long flat thing that squirmed like a worm. So if ham that came from a pig, I pondered, could cultivate in your stomach an ugly thing like that, perhaps sausage that came from a horse could…

"Sit down everyone…dinner is served." Mutti brought the sizzling pan to the table. *Vati* was the first to be served. While *Mutti* served the rest of us, my eyes were on *Vati*. I loved to watch him eat. His etiquette at the table competed with the etiquette of Queen Elizabeth of England. His hands, calloused and never quite rid of iron grit under the fingernails, manipulated with greatest finesse his fork and knife. With the fork in his left hand, he delicately pricked the sausage, making it ooze. With the knife in his right hand, he delicately carved a small piece off. In the European fashion, without putting down the knife, he delicately brought the fork, still held in his left hand, to his mouth. He closed his eyes, savoring the taste. "Mm-m-m…*lecker*," he proclaimed at last. "Come, come…start eating." He gestured with his chin to the food.

My eyes wandered from *Vati* to my cousin. The shadow of his beard gave Hans a manly air. As he munched with gusto, there was a touch of humor around his mouth. When he caught me watching him, with my brows drawn together in reservation, he gave me the wait and see, soon we'll neigh look.

Ach, I thought, he's just teasing me. Even if not, the nice old doctor with the silver hair and silver goatee, the one who had a remedy for the tapeworm malady, most likely will have a remedy for this too, for the neighing, that is. Overcome by hunger pangs, no longer able to resist the luscious aroma, I heaved a sigh, licked my lips, and gingerly took a bite. It was heavenly. The only sound was the sound of food being scraped off plates, set to the background of a Mozart symphony.

30

  The *Stieffmütterchen* nodded in the breeze and greeted me with a smile. *Frau* Fischer, Rosemarie's mother, must have had this in mind, I thought, when she planted the pansies along the entrance walk, leading to their whitewashed stucco house. I marveled at the flowers' beautiful faces, and wondered why they were called stepmothers, the German translation of the English word pansies.
  Rosemarie Fischer was a classmate and friend. I climbed the steps, knocked on the door, and waited. The melody of *Eine feste Burg ist unser Gott* carried on the wind up the hill to my ears, now thunderous, now soft, depending on the direction of the air-current. It was Sunday morning and, no sooner had the church bells stopped ringing, the brass ensemble started to play familiar church hymns from atop the *Marktkirchturm*.
  Rosemarie opened the door. "Want to go to the cemetery with my *Opa* and me?" Her big brown eyes, beneath curly chestnut bangs, waited for an answer.
  "*Ja*," I said, stepping through the open door. "I would like that." We never went to church, except on Christmas and Easter, and I guessed the Fischers did not either, so the cemetery seemed to be a good

substitute, just in case God was keeping track. Besides, I recalled the last time Rosmarie's grandfather took us for a hike in the forest, we had great fun learning how to identify every tree, every chirp of every bird, and every name and shape of every cloud.

"I never had an *Opa*. Did you know that?" I said, my voice hinting at regret. I liked Rosemarie's grandfather, a judicious looking old man with an abundance of white hair.

"How come? Everyone has grandfathers."

"*Ja*, but mine died before I was born."

Rosemarie pulled me into the living room. Her eyes told me she sympathized. "You mean they died young?"

"*Ja*, my Opa Machein fell off a wagon while pitching hay. He cracked his skull wide open."

"*Autsch*." Rosemarie grimaced in pain.

"My *Opa* Holder died in the trenches of World War I."

"How do you know that?"

"I heard my grandmother tell my mother once, that's what happened. You know drowned in the mud in the trenches they dug to fight the British and the French."

"War stinks." My friend's eyes clouded with sadness.

"I know," I agreed. "My father was just a little boy when World War I was over. When the soldiers returned, he'd sit on the front stoop and, searching each passing soldier's face, he'd ask, 'Are you my Dad?' That's what I heard my grandmother say."

"That's so sad." Rosemarie sagged against the door.

"*Ja*. For days he cut school to make sure he'd be there to welcome him back…but he never came home, my father's father, that is."

"War is so stupid, I think." Rosemarie said. "Did you know that Jutta's father was extradited to France?" Jutta, a classmate, was Rosemarie's other friend. "I think he's never coming back, either."

auf Wiedersehen

Rosemarie lowered her voice so as not to be overheard should any one enter the room.

"How come...? What's extradited...?" I was curious.

"Some Americans...maybe British...I can't remember what Jutta told me...I think, maybe, they were French...took him back to France." Rosemarie ironed the crease between her eyes with her index and middle fingers.

"Why did they take him back to France?"

"Because that's where he was stationed during the war. I think he was an SS...you know Gestapo, and he did bad things to people there. Now he has to stand trial for war crimes he committed."

"What did he do?" I asked, trying to remember what I heard from other classmates.

"Jutta didn't tell me. She thinks her father is being unjustly persecuted."

Rosemarie's mother walked into the living room then, holding a cup of coffee in her hand. "*Guten Morgen*, Christa." She picked up a book from the side table and headed for the plush velvety armchair. The rich aroma of fresh-brewed coffee followed her. "Nice you came to visit us."

Frau Fischer, dressed in a turquoise dressing gown, was an attractive Woman, slender and of medium height, she had eyes like a doe, and wavy chestnut hair, not at all like the typical plain, big-boned German *Hausfrau*. Like all German *Hausfrauen*, her life was centered on her family, on her home, and on her garden. *Herr* Fischer, a corpulent man, the editor of the only newspaper in town, was a prominent citizen of the community. Rosemarie's older brother, her only sibling, attended the *Hochschule*, the one Rosel soon would attend. One had to be smart and take an entrance exam to get in. It puzzled me that some of the most dim-witted kids in town were able to pass the entrance exam, as for instance the baker's daughter, the butcher's son, and the...

"So are you two going with *Opa* to the cemetery?" *Frau* Fischer's question cut into my thoughts. She picked up her cup and took a sip of the aromatic coffee.

I pictured *Mutti* sitting at home, on a hard wooden chair, holding a tin cup of *Ersatz Kaffee* in her hands, hands turned red from scrubbing iron grime from morning to night. One day, I wowed, you'll have a plush armchair like this, and I'll serve you real coffee in a Dresden porcelain cup.

~ * ~

The cemeteries in Germany, as everything else, were tended to with utmost care. Flowers bloomed in all shades on every grave, without so much as a single sliver of weed allowed to sprout.

"Your *Opa* must miss your *Oma* a lot." I watched the old man kneeling at the grave, trying to imagine what it must be like to lose someone close to you. He was digging in the dirt, smiling, and mumbling softly to the gravestone.

"*Ja*," I think he can't wait to be with her again…I think he can't wait to die, which makes me so mad." Rosemarie turned to me, looking more sad than angry.

"Why?" I asked, thinking it was nice to want to be reunited with your loved one in a life hereafter, sort of romantic.

"Because I love him too." Rosemarie pursed her lips. "I want him to stay with me…I love going for long walks with him through the forest. Do you want to come next Saturday with us?"

"Sure," I said, hoping the wild boars we encountered on our last hike through the woods, would long be gone. "I'll have to ask my mother, though."

auf Wiedersehen

When the old man finished tending to his wife's grave, he walked to a nearby tree, which shadowed a bench. He sat down and rested his weary head on his hands, one clasped over the other on top of the arc of his walking stick.

"Come on," Rosemarie pulled my arm. "Let's go and see who can find the oldest gravestone." We marveled at every long life we discovered, grieved for every short one, and laughed out loud at funny names.

When the wind began to lament, and the sun slid behind heavy rain clouds, we headed for home. "Don't forget we're going on a hike next Saturday," Rosemarie shouted, waving good-bye.

"I won't," I replied, starting to walk in the opposite direction toward my home. "If it's nice tomorrow, will you come swimming?"

"*Ja*," Rosemarie yelled back. "Meet you at the swimming pool."

Swimming pool, swimming pool, the echo traveled over the valley and brought to surface the story I heard about our classmate's father, who had to stand trial in France for atrocities he committed there during the war. Like a volcano the scene, as it must have been, erupted in my brain.

A group of Jews, under his guard, had been herded to a swimming pool for cleansing purposes. Dressed in his tidy SS uniform, the classmate's father stood on top of the platform of the high diving board. One by one, as each wretched, dejected soul had been forced to climb the narrow ladder by another SS man, he taunted them as they inched forward to the edge. With his shiny black knee-high boot, whether they could swim or not, he kicked them into the dark abyss.

31

A swallow perched on her nest under the overhang. She fluffed her feathers against the wind, then snuggled her young ones beneath her. I entered the horses' quarters and looked into the dark stalls. Ludwig was there, but Lotte's stall was still empty. She should have been back by now. I knew, of course, she had not been well and needed medical attention. Still, that was a while ago. I wondered where they took her.

"Where's Lotte?" I asked when Otto emerged from the rear. I longed to hear the sound of her hoofs clumpety-clumping across the cobblestone yard. "When is she coming back?"

Avoiding my eyes, Otto mumbled something unintelligible. He picked up the pitchfork and, at a frantic pace, he fluffed up the straw around Ludwig's legs. "Run along now," he barked. "I have a lot to do…I have no time for chitchat today."

A sense of foreboding sent shivers down my spine. It was not like Otto to brush me off. Otto had never been unkind. I scurried next door, up the three steps, and burst into our kitchen just in time to hear *Vati* say, "but she'll find out sooner or later that…" biting his lip, his eyes caught hold of mine, and he stopped in mid-sentence.

auf Wiedersehen

"Who'll find out what?" I glanced from *Vati* to *Mutti*. "Are you talking about me?"

"*Nein, nein...*" *Mutti* stirred uneasily in her chair. Fumbling with her apron ends, she said, "We were just talking about the letter that came from the *Auswanderung Amt*...it looks like all the papers are in order...it looks like we are really going to America, *ist das nicht wunderbar?*" She looked at me with those sapphire eyes that showed the sensitivity of a mother. "All we have to do now is wait until we get the final approval from the American immigration bureau."

Rosel, her nose buried in a book, pretended to read. Her fingers on the page fluttered like butterfly wings and tears rolled down her flushed cheek.

"Why are you crying?" I asked. "Is it because you don't want to go to America...is it because you'll miss your friends?"

Rosel shook her head from side to side and dabbed at her eyes.

Darkness pressed down on me then, for I sensed why everyone was acting so strange. I sensed it. I felt it. I knew it.

"Lotte is dead, isn't she?" I cried, a war of emotion raging within me.

No one dared to answer me.

"It was Lotte...and we...and why didn't you...?" I gasped for air.

Mutti got up then and, reaching out, caught my hand. I pulled away, ran outside, and collapsed on the top step. Silence loomed across the iron works yard. It was late Sunday afternoon. All the ironworkers were at home. The Romanians from next door, most likely, were still at the soccer game. There were no happy neighs coming from the horses' quarters. All was still. Ludwig was mourning Lotte. The rich aroma of venison stew drifted across the yard from the main house, the proprietor's house, Burchard's house. How generous of him to divide Lotte into six sausages for each ironworker. I hated his guts.

I hated Otto for not telling me Lotte had been killed. I hated *Vati*, who lately just shrugged at everything. I hated Rosel for crying, Lotte had not been her friend. I hated *Mutti* for all my woes. I hated the world. Most of all, I hated myself for I could not deny the lingering good taste of…my bones turned to ashes at the thought. I blinked at the sun that peeked out from behind a cloud, and whimpered, "How can you be so bright when I feel black like thunder?"

32

Seasons came and seasons passed, and life in Osterode went on while we waited for the final okay from the American authorities.

The communists adorned tunnels and walls with Ami go home slogans. We waited.

A local girl, jilted by her lover, threw herself in front of an onrushing train. From then on she was seen around town, without legs, in a wheelchair. We waited.

The Americans and British stripped the surrounding forests and shipped the logs home. We waited.

We went to the cinema, once. Although we saved every *Pfennig* for our trip to America, *Mutti* allowed us to splurge when, *Wir Reisen nach Amerika* played, and we all went to see the film. From then on, anticipation grew. We waited.

Somewhere in Germany, a German shot a German entangled in barbed wire while crossing from Germany to Germany. We waited.

Fräulein Gertrud brought, hidden under her apron, ice-skates she found in the boss' attic. We skated, and we waited.

Then one day in early June of 1951, a day when even the air seemed to be holding its breath, the final word came, everything was in order.

~ * ~

"The train will take us to Hamburg," *Mutti* explained. "In Hamburg we'll take a train to Rotterdam. There we will board the ship that will take us to New York."

"Did you know The *Nieuw* Amsterdam is Holland's second largest ship?" Rosel asked, in a voice oddly mixed with excitement and anxiety.

"How do you know?" I moved closer to her, my head thrust forward. Rosel, not yet sixteen, was a sight to be seen with her long braided golden hair, pale blue eyes with a splash of green, and budding boobs.

"I looked it up, *Dummkopf*." She nudged my head back with her fingertips. "It's one of the world's finest and most luxurious ships. It has swimming pools, restaurants, theaters, and little shops, just like a city block."

"*Toll...*" I was impressed, and hoped it wouldn't sink. "It'll be so...so... fantastic to swim in a pool on top of the Atlantic."

"I'm not sure you can," *Mutti* interjected. "We're going third class, you know. I doubt there's a swimming pool for third class passengers."

"Don't worry." *Vati* grinned. "We'll find a way to get to the pool. I know my way around ships...a ship has many gangways, and one will lead us to the pool." He slapped his thigh with the palm of his hand.

In spite of herself, *Mutti* chuckled. "I see it coming, you'll get us thrown off the ship, and we can all go swimming, in the Atlantic, that is."

Vati turned his grin up a notch and went on cheerfully. "Or maybe, we'll swim in the first-class pool, what do you say to that?"

~ * ~

We barely had enough time to say *auf Wiedersehen* to friends and neighbors, pack our few belongings, and scrub every inch, once more, to assure cleanliness would welcome the next inhabitants.

For more than five years, here we'd lived in these two rooms, separated by a plaster- chipped wall from the horses' stalls. Here, *Vati* worked, across the yard, in the dark pit over an orange fire, while his face slowly turned yellow, and the depth of laughter in his eyes grew shallow. Here, *Mutti* fought to have us walk with pride in a hopeless place. Day in day out, she washed and scrubbed, against the steadfast will of grime and iron dust. She arranged wildflowers and lit tall candles at dinnertime. She placed Goethe, Schiller, and Mark Twain on the bookshelf. Here, while never abandoning the dream of a better life in America, she turned these ghastly two rooms into a home, where Rosel and I could bring our friends. Here, we laughed, cried, and harmonized many a night in song, for more than five years.

"Are you ready?" Hans panted his way through the kitchen door. "I was afraid I'd be late and miss you." He smoothed back an abundance of black hair with his hand.

"Are you coming with us?" My words ran together excitedly, hope against hope.

"*Nein, nein*, I wish I could…but I just came to see you off." He turned to *Mutti* then, and gestured to the two suitcases and two smaller bags in the middle of the floor. "Is this all the luggage you have?"

"*Ja*, Hans." Mutti nodded decisively. "We're ready. *Ja*, this is all we have." Drawing her brows downward, she asked, "Are your mother and sister not coming to the station with us?"

"*Ja*, of course…they're waiting by the gate."

"Well then, let's go." *Vati* picked up the two suitcases and almost collapsed from the weight.

"*Onkel* Martin, let me carry that." Hans took the suitcases from my dad and walked outdoors, ahead of us, and *Vati* picked up the two lighter bags.

Tante Lieschen and Bienchen came walking toward us just as we passed the horse's quarter. Ludwig neighed as if to say *auf Wiedersehen*. And the swallows swooshed low, in front and in back, and all around us too.

We stood in the gates of the iron-works yard and looked, for the very last time, at the tall chimney spewing flames toward the darkening sky. Carrying all our worldly possessions, we stepped through the gates, leaving the shadows of our hearts behind, and taking along only the sun.

"*Na Du*…" Hans gave me a slight nudge in my ribs. Tilting his head, his eyes strangely veiled, he gave me a sideways glance. "I hope you'll write," his husky voice urged.

"*Ja*…I will." Skipping a pace, I fell in step beside him. Although, at thirteen, I no longer nurtured a puppy crush, I still thought he was the handsomest man alive. I wondered what kind of woman he'd fall in love with someday. Someone nice I hoped. Through quivering lips I repeated, "*Ja*, I will write."

"I hope you don't get seasick." Bienchen bounced up to my sister. She put one arm around Rosel's shoulders and squeezed her affectionately. Bienchen had fallen in love with a local young man, named Herbert Mai. He was tall, handsome, and an engineer, but I

auf Wiedersehen

hoped she would not marry him. He was too snobbish, too lifeless, too unyielding, I thought, for our bubbly Bienchen.

With long purposeful strides, carrying a bag in each hand, *Vati* walked grandly ahead of us all. "Hurry up," he shouted over his shoulder. "I see it coming, we'll miss the train."

Tante Lieschen, walking behind us shoulder to shoulder with *Mutti*, spoke in a tear-smothered voice. "At least I no longer will have to put up with your cheating at games. I no longer will have to endure Christa's make-up attempts."

"I will miss our games." *Mutti* cleared her throat. "I will miss you, dear sister."

I turned around and looked at them. *Mutti's* composure, I could see, was under attack. *Tante* Lieschen, white as snow, lowered her long black lashes against a stream of tears.

What a strange sight we were, happy and sad, marching down the street, two by two. I concentrated on my feet, methodically bringing one in front of the other. My shoes were hand-me-downs, but *Vati* polished them like new.

"In America, you won't have to wear my old stuff." Rosel tried to cheer me up. "In America, we'll both get a new wardrobe, I bet."

"*Ja*, and we'll live in a mansion by the river, don't forget," I had thrown in, wrapped in a silken cocoon of euphoric anticipation.

So we marched on, each to our own thoughts. The sky turned dark violet, and the wind, gently following, carried forth the sound of church bells tolling, fare-thee-well.

33

"*Ja-a-a…*" said the travel agent behind the counter, smiling with cool confidence. "I have your tickets…but they are for cabin class…not tourist class."

"It can't be…" *Mutti's* eyes widened in alarm "It must be a mistake. We booked for tourist class."

"*Nein*…you can see right here, it says Holder, party of four, cabin class." He swiveled the book around and tapped his index finger on a line half way down the page. "See?"

Having confirmed that, indeed, it said cabin class, *Mutti* half turned and looked at *Vati*. "What do we do now? We only have enough money for tourist class."

Vati stepped up to the counter then, and in a tone of voice one might use to reprimand a small child, he said, "I'll have you know young man, we have waited five years to get the damned immigration papers in order, and we are waiting no longer." He raised his hand to silence the agent, who attempted to interrupt him. "We came straight here from the train station to pick up our tickets." *Vati* gestured to the bags. "We have to catch another train that will take us to Holland where we'll board our ship. As you can imagine, we are tired, and we will not put up with this nonsense. So run along." He shooed the man with a flip of his hand. "Run along and see what you can do."

Unimpressed, the young man didn't budge. He cleared his throat and said, "There's absolutely nothing that I can do. His smug expression revealed an air of contempt.

Throwing up his hands, *Vati* sighed.

The agent tilted his head and looked past *Vati*. "Please be so kind and step aside. Others are waiting."

Mutti took hold of *Vati's* arm, and pulled him to where Rosel and I stood, guarding our luggage.

"What can we do?" Rosel's eyes bore into *Mutti*.

With her shoulders drooping, and her arms hanging lamely at her sides, *Mutti* shrugged. "I don't know," she murmured.

An elderly lady, with the aid of a cane, walked into the travel bureau, letting in momentarily, the hum of the city. Hamburg, the gate of Europe, as it is sometimes referred to, still showed the devastation of the war. Through the large display window I could see many buildings in ruin.

"I don't know," *Mutti* repeated, her voice drifting into a whisper. I studied my mother and looked for that familiar gleam of strength, but when I couldn't find it in her eyes, I squeezed mine shut and prayed as I had never prayed before. *Dear God, I do believe that you exist, and I do believe in miracles, so wont you please perform one now?* I squeezed my eyes even tighter then, until a light began to flash inside my head. My blood pounded, my skin burned, and every nerve in my body prickled. *It must be God*, I thought, *answering*. When, at last, I opened my eyes again, I saw no money floating our way, and so I asked, no one in particular this time, "Can't we borrow what we need?"

"Of course," *Vati* agreed readily. "We'll have to borrow the money, but from whom? Who could lend it to us?" He scratched his head and his eyes clung to *Mutti*, analyzing her reaction, knowing all too well she was too proud to ask anyone for anything. "How about your sister?" Vati suggested.

"Where would she get it from?" Shaking her head, *Mutti* turned from him without waiting for an answer. She focused her eyes on a picture hanging on the wall behind the counter. There she was displayed in all her glory, the S.S. Nieuw Amsterdam, with her two slanted chimneystacks, our ship. *Mutti* turned back to *Vati*. "You must know Lieschen has no money to spare."

"What about Paul Westendorf, our rich friend?" I piped in.

"She's right." *Vati* beamed. "He could telegraph us the money." His words rang with excitement. "If he would, we could still catch the ship in time. Do you think he would?"

Mutti threw her shoulders back and, through tight lips, she said, "*Nein*. Out of the question. We can't ask him, he's helped us too much already."

"Exactly, he'll help us again." Oblivious of the other travelers staring, *Vati* turned up the volume of his voice, and pushed the words at her. "Don't be a stubborn Prussian now…don't ruin everything…I beg you, we've come too far." He grabbed her shoulders and tried to shake off that damn Prussian pride.

Even Rosel agreed, perhaps, *Vati* was right. Perhaps it would be all right to ask *Onkel* Paul, our friend.

Mutti, with her lips clamped together and a deep furrow between her eyes, stood very still for a very long time. At last, making an awkward sound, she swallowed her pride and, in a low tormented voice, she said, "All right."

She turned to the agent behind the counter then, and raising her chin, she assumed all the dignity she could muster, and shouted "Young man…hold those tickets for us… we'll be back." Picking up the two smaller bags, she headed for the door and urged, "We have to hurry…we have to find a public phone and make the call. Hurry, hurry, *kommt, macht schnell*."

34

A fog obscured Rotterdam. Through the silence of dawn, a ship blasted its farewell, low and sad.

"*Um Gottes Willen*...I hope it's not our ship." *Mutti*, weighted down with baggage, increased the pace of her walk to a run. "Hurry, hurry, we're almost there."

Rosel on the left of *Vati*, and I on the right, tugged at our suitcases as we stumbled behind her.

~ * ~

When *Mutti* reached *Onkel* Paul by telephone, the day after the mix-up with the tickets, and advised him of our predicament, he didn't hesitate and telegraphed the appropriate sum overnight. While we waited for the money to arrive, we stayed in one of several barracks located on the outskirts of Hamburg. Countless people, homeless since the war, were stranded there. We were lucky. We only had to stay two nights. I was convinced the way things fell into place was almost like a miracle, and it was the direct result of my appeal to God.

Almost a miracle, that is, for we still had to get to the ship in time. The foghorn blasted yet again, much louder now. The scent of the sea became more intense.

At last, we reached the long wet dock. No sooner did we struggle up the gangplank, than it was drawn in. A sigh of relief escaped *Mutti's* lips, as we nearly collapsed on deck.

Through tear-bordered eyes I saw a tall figure, like an angel in white, approach.

"Let me help you with that." A dapper officer, dressed in a crisp uniform, picked up our two bags. "Follow me…I'll show you to your stateroom." The warmth of his smile echoed in his voice. "This way…I'll have someone bring your other luggage later."

As soon as the kindly officer left our room, *Mutti* fell into a plush armchair. Her hands flew up to her cheeks. Her eyes took in the pleasing color scheme of eggshell tones that gave our cabin an air of quiet distinction. She turned to *Vati,* her expression still and somber. "It's almost as if we were back home…back home in Görlitz."

Vati nodded, letting his eyes roam all around the ample room. He dropped down on the floor beside her, and faced her. "From now on, life will get only better. I promise you."

They shared a smile, and *Mutti* stroked his head.

"We have our own private bathroom," Rosel exclaimed, disappearing through a door. "Can you believe that?"

I followed her and buried my face in one of the huge white towels. "*Toll,*" I exclaimed. "Feel how soft. Smell this soap." I held a bar under her nose.

Rosel, with her arms crossed, took a whiff and agreed, "It smells really nice."

"*Ja*, it doesn't stink like castile soap." It smells like a rose, don't you think?"

She just smiled. Uncrossing her arms she tore off a sheet of toilet paper and fingered it. "Feel how soft this is," she murmured handing it to me.

"*Toll.*" I inspected the tissue with my thumb and two fingers. "No more sore Popo."

Vati peeked into the bathroom then. "Who is first to soak in the bath?"

~ * ~

Three hours later and smelling like roses, we went in search of the dining room. Two young stewards, anxious to please, were assigned to our table.

"May I suggest the smoked salmon served on a bed of crisp lettuce?" The taller one asked.

"Perhaps the girls would prefer a cheeseburger with Pommes frites?" The shorter one inquired. The point of my tongue moistened my upper lip.

"Perhaps you would like…?" It went on and on, and the décor in the Dining Salon enhanced the lavish continental cuisine.

After the meal, we went in search of the swimming pool. The gleaming mosaic-tiled pool was filled with real ocean water and beckoned to us.

"What are you waiting for?" *Vati* looked at me. "Let's go and get our bathing suits."

All during the voyage, the air-conditioned theatre with its dramatically colorful portieres, showed first-run films. It didn't cost anything.

The highlight of the ship was the vast deck. Here we promenaded each day, soaked up the warm June sun, and watched the fish jump over whitecaps. It was 1951, we were at last on our way to America, where a new life awaited us. I was thirteen, too young, too ignorant to have been aware of other ships that, not too long ago, crossed these same waters carrying people with the same dreams of a new life in America.

~ * ~

One such ship was the SS Navemar, a Spanish freighter equipped to carry twenty-eight passengers. In 1941, one thousand Jews were crammed into its cargo holds. Over a half-million dollars in passage money was paid on this ship. Yet conditions on board were intolerable. Old men and women lying listless on their bunks gasping for air in the excruciating heat, lice infested children restless and crying, and everyone hungry, thirsty, dirty, the smell of urine and feces permeating the ship, the ship bound for nowhere, for entry was denied first in Cuba, then in the US. The free world, once again, had answered their cries for help with extortion, with deception, with rejection.

~ * ~

On the seventh day of our journey, at the crack of dawn, *Mutti* woke us up. "Hurry and get dressed. We have arrived. Let's go on deck."

We squeezed between other passengers by the railing. "*Guten Morgen*," *Vati* in elated mood, greeted everyone. Everyone watched as two tugboats approached and, after they made contact with the SS Nieuw Amsterdam, masterfully maneuvered us into the harbor.

"Look," *Vati* pointed toward the New York skyline where, edged against the rising sun, buildings, tall like I had never seen before, reached for the sky. None were in ruins.

"No bombs ever fell here?" I asked in astonishment. "Never?"

auf Wiedersehen

"No, dummy. Hitler didn't reach this far." Rosel poked her elbow into my side. "Look over there." She half turned and pointed in the opposite direction. "Look, The Statue of Liberty…See how she holds her torch to welcome us?"

"I know," I said in a tone of importance. "I learned about the Lady in English class …the Lady of Freedom." I looked at my sister waiting for her approval. "I also know what's inscribed on her, really I do."

"Can you recite it in English then?" Rosel raised one eyebrow.

"Sure." I nodded my head. "Well, not all of it, but part of it."

"Say the part I like," *Mutti* joined in. "You know, Christa, the part you translated for me once. I love those words. Do you still remember them?"

"You mean, Giff me your tired, your poor, your huddled masses yearning to breed free, the wretched refuse of your teeming shore. Send dese, de homeless, tempest-tossed to me, I lift my lamp beside de golden door."

"*Ja*, that's the part." *Mutti* smiled as we sailed past the lady through the golden door.

"Hm…" Rosel smiled too. "You'll have to work on that accent I think, or people will call you dumb German Kraut."

"What about your accent…it's even worse," I shot back in defense. Then more calmly I asked, "What does refuse mean, Rosel?"

"Refuse is *Abfall*, you know garbage."

"So if she welcomes us, why does she refer to us as garbage?" I wondered out loud.

"No, no," Rosel's voice was full of disdain. "It can also mean…"

"Girls, we have to go below. Look, we're here, the tug boats are pushing us toward a dock." *Mutti* pulled us away from the railing.

Rosel stood rigid and grabbed the railing with both hands. "Our port of arrival is Hoboken. This is not Hoboken. This is an island.

Hoboken should be on the west side of the harbor." She turned around and pointed to the other side. "It should be over there in New Jersey."

Vati, impressed by his daughter's vast knowledge, smiled with pride.

She was right. The ship made a brief stop at Ellis Island where a few passengers who, during the crossing had taken ill, were quarantined. This accomplished, the tugboats chugged us away from the dock and steered the ship's bow toward the other side, toward Hoboken with its much less imposing skyline, to where Paul Westendorf, our sponsor and millionaire friend, was waiting for us.

35

There was an air of shyness about Paul Westendorf, as he stood there, his legs slightly apart, and his fingers buried in his threadbare blazer pockets. He was trim rather than tall, and his dress was simple but neat. His eyes considered each disembarking passenger until they caught and held *Mutti's*. He had a pale, sensitive face, and his dark hair, just graying at the temples, was still full. He managed a tentative smile as he walked to the gangplank.

"Welcome to America." He extended his hand to *Mutti*.

Mutti enclosed his hand with both of hers and held on tight. "Paul, it's been so very long. You look...you look...you look fabulous. I would have recognized you anywhere."

I could see that she lied. Mutti never lied. She always said the way things were. Black was black, and white was white. Still, as I watched the play of emotion on her face, I could have sworn she'd just lied. Was she disappointed as I, I wondered? Uncle Paul did not look anything like the debonair rich American I envisioned. At last *Mutti* withdrew her hands, and said, "Paul, I'd like you to meet my husband. This is Martin. This is my oldest child, Rosel. This is Christa."

Paul shook hands with each one of us, and each time his eyes reflected glimmers of warmth. "You can call me *Onkel* Paul," he told Rosel and me. Turning to *Mutti*, he asked, "What would you like to do…we have a few hours before our train leaves. Perhaps you'd like to visit the Statue of Liberty?"

We collected our baggage and stored it in a locker, and walked to the ferry not far from where we docked.

~ * ~

"You don't look so good, Rosel." I put my hand on her shoulder. Her head drooped to her chest and her body slumped over the ferry's railing. "Are you all right?"

Rosel heaved a few times then vomited her heart out.

Mutti looked concerned as she wiped Rosel's face with a handkerchief, and the crowd of visitors who had come to see the Lady of Freedom, edged away from us. "She didn't get sea-sick crossing the Atlantic with waves up to ten feet high," *Vati* let *Onkel* Paul know. "Here, where the water is like a mirror…look at her, poor thing…she's white as a ghost."

"Perhaps we should go and sit down." *Onkel* Paul pointed to a space on a bench. His eyes were full of concern.

"I'll be fine." Rosel could hardly lift her voice above a whisper. "Really, I'll be fine…don't fuss."

"She's not used to so much excitement…so many people." *Mutti* apologized to her friend. Her eyes rested on the crowd at the railing, eagerly chatting and pointing to the Statue of Liberty.

"She'll like it in Nichols then." *Onkel* Paul gave Rosel that little tentative smile of his. "Nichols is a quiet, peaceful town."

auf Wiedersehen

We huffed and we puffed and climbed the steps, all three hundred and fifty four of them, up to the crown of the Statue of Liberty. We marveled at the magnificence of New York Harbor, lingering for a little while, and then descended the same steps, all three hundred and fifty four of them. By the time we stepped out onto the deck of the Lady, it was time to head for the train, the train that was to take us to Nichols, upstate New York, our new home.

~ * ~

Nichols, a small sleepy cow town, was bordered on one side by sloping hills, and on the other side by the Susquehanna River, and in between stretched the fields around dairy farms. We pulled off the main road and drove along a dirt path winding its way through sprouting corn plants. *Onkel* Paul's car, not a Cadillac but some sort of an antique, stalled a few times. "If you give me a push," Uncle Paul said each time, "I can get her started again." We scrambled out of the car, pushed until the motor sputtered back to life, jumped back into the car and sput-sput-sput-sputted on. At last we arrived at Onkel Paul's mansion by the river.

Shaded by tall trees, stood a small cabin. It must be the caretaker's place, I thought, and let my eyes roam in search of the big house.

"This way," *Onkel* Paul gestured toward the cabin. We climbed a few steps and entered two rooms, dark and filled with a musty scent of a hermit's existence. *Onkel* Paul pointed to a door. "You can sleep there. I will sleep here." There consisted of two metal beds, a dresser, and some folded cots. Here consisted of an antique stove, a couch, a table, some chairs, and lots and lots of books stacked in the corner on the floor guarded by a tri-colored tomcat, that hissed as if ready to attack.

As it turned out, *Onkel* Paul was a devout member of the Pentecostal church, and gave all his money to various charities. To possess material things he considered a sin. After we collected ourselves, he invited us to join him in prayer. After much coaxing and pulling on *Mutti's* part, Rosel and I fell to our knees and closed the gap in the circle of prayer.

"Dear Lord, we are gathered here in gratitude…we thank you for uniting us…we thank you for the bountiful blessings you have bestowed on us…we thank you for our riches…" and so it went on and on. At last *Onkel* Paul stopped, and walked outside.

We scrambled off the floor, and stared at each other, our lips clamped. A look of amusement entered *Vati's* eyes and a chuckle escaped him.

"Sh-h-h," *Mutti* put her finger over her lips. "He'll hear you," she whispered. "We mustn't hurt his feelings." Her eyes roamed around the bleakness of our surroundings. "Do not forget how much he has helped us. He has made it possible for us to come to America, and in America all things are achievable."

That hypothesis did not help Rosel. She looked absolutely miserable. I looked around and discovered, there was no electricity. A kerosene lantern stood on the bare table. There was no sink, but through the window I saw a pump. Beyond the pump was an outhouse, our own private outhouse. Now that was definitely a step up for us, an outhouse all to ourselves. I walked outside.

~ * ~

Through the flickering shade of trees I saw *Onkel* Paul at water's edge. I walked up to him, quietly, so as not to disturb the tranquility.

"Listen," he said over his shoulder. "Hear?"

auf Wiedersehen

For a moment I only heard the rustling of reeds, the lapping of water against the shore, but then a sound so sweet and yet so sad drifted across the river. I tilted my head to one side and looked at him.

"It's a loon," he said. His voice was tender, almost a murmur.

The sun spilled its golden glow as it sank into the Susquehanna. "Look," *Onkel* Paul pointed. "See?"

A boat chugged lazily upstream leaving behind a luminous wake on the river growing still.

I slipped my hand through the crook of his arm and whispered, "I think I'm going to like it here."

About the Author

Christa Holder Ocker, a #1 New York Times best-selling contributing author, began to write short stories and poems after years of domestic doldrums. Her story, "Merry Christmas, my Friend", translated in many languages, was adapted for TV and starred Mickey Rooney. She loves writing, sailing, skiing, and frolicking with her twelve incredible grandkids. ockerc@gmail.com

**VISIT OUR WEBSITE
FOR THE FULL INVENTORY
OF QUALITY BOOKS**:

http://www.roguephoenixpress.com

Representing Excellence in Publishing

*Quality trade paperbacks and downloads
in multiple formats,
in genres ranging from historical to contemporary romance,
mystery and science fiction.
Visit the website then bookmark it.
We add new titles each month!*

www.ingramcontent.com/pod-product-compliance
Lightning Source LLC
Chambersburg PA
CBHW061326040426
42444CB00011B/2793